KULILKATIMA

KULILKATIMA
SEEKING UNDERSTANDING

Ted Egan

KERR

Melbourne, Victoria

First published 2022
Kerr Publishing Pty Ltd
Melbourne, Victoria
ABN 64 124 219 638

© 2022 Ted Egan

This book is copyright. Unless stated otherwise, all images are included in the above copyright. Apart from fair dealing for the purpose of private study, research, criticism or review, or under the Copyright Agency Ltd rules of recording, no part may be reproduced by any means.

The moral right of the author has been asserted.

ISBN 978-1-875703-50-0 (PoD, Print on Demand)

Cover and book design: Paul Taylder of Xigrafix Media and Design

Typeset in Caslon Pro 11/15pt

Print-on-Demand services: Lightning Source

National Library of Australia PrePublication Data Service:

 A catalogue record for this book is available from the National Library of Australia

Dedication

Kulilkatima: Seeking Understanding

This book is dedicated to the following great Australians, all of whom have had a benign and profound influence on my long and happy life:

    Grace and Joe Egan, my dear parents
    Nerys Evans, my CFL
    Pat, Peg, Shirley Tim, my aff. siblings
    Aloysius Puantulura
    Edward Condon Evans—"Ted Heaven"
    Fred Gray
    Ms Beulah Lowe
    H C 'Nugget' Coombs
    Narritjin Maymuru
    Munggurawuy Yunupingu
    Vincent Lingiari
    Raphael Apuatimi OAM

Contents

1	My Right to Write	1
2	The Republic	5
3	New Regional Centres	11
4	The New Flag	17
5	The Economy Post-Covid	19
6	National Service	23
7	Australia: A World Force	27
8	Two Academies	31
9	Elimination of Drought	35
10	Bushfires	43
11	Cars and Car Parks	49
12	The First Australians	53
13	Mutual Recognition	63
14	Full Nationhood	73
15	The Language known as Australian?	77
16	Wealth for First Australian Nations	85
17	Funding the Arts	97
18	Health and Education	105
19	The Health of First Australians	113
20	The Education of First Australians	127
21	Aged Care	133
22	Attitudes to Gender	135
23	Summary and Conclusion	141

1 My Right to Write

> ## This Land Australia
>
> Kulilkatima
> Ngura nyangatja
> Irititjanya
> Putula, kulinyi
> Nguntju nganampa
> Kililya win'kitja
> Uru pulunta ngaranyi
>
> Try to understand
> This land Australia
> Take her as she is
> Her moods, her mysteries
> Mother of us all
> Beneath the Southern Cross
> In her frame of peaceful seas
>
> The shimmer of the midday haze
> On endless inland plains
> The busy city's bustling pace,
> The drenching, life filled rains

> Try to understand, this land Australia
> Take her as she is, her moods, her mysteries
> Mother of us all, beneath the Southern Cross
> In her frame of peaceful seas
>
> The lustre of the Barrier Reef
> The snow clad Alps on high.
> The fires, the floods, the searing droughts
> Just love her, don't ask why
>
> Yes, try to understand, this land Australia
> Take her as she is, her moods her mysteries
> Mother of us all, beneath the Southern Cross
> In her frame of peaceful seas.
>
> The tribal stories, ages old
> The deeds of pioneers
> The way of life we proudly hold
> The triumph and the tears.
>
> Try to understand, my land Australia
> Take her as she is, her moods her mysteries
> Mother of us all, beneath the Southern Cross
> In her frame of peaceful seas.
>
> *Words and Music: Ted Egan (1988)*

I AM TED EGAN, THE SON OF GRACE BRENNAN (B. 1901) AND Joe Egan (b. 1898), both born on farms in western Victoria, Australia. My parents were married in 1922, enjoying—at the time—better than average affluence, in that they had the money for a substantial deposit on a new home in Coburg, Melbourne, Victoria. In the 1930s they—like so many others—were brutalised by the economic Depression that besieged the entire western world. Joe was out of permanent work from 1932–1939: for much of the time he was 'on the susso'—today called the dole. He rode his bicycle ten miles each day to seek work. He struck an agreement with his bank to pay sixpence (6d) a week against his mortgage, eventually settling the debt. Grace was a competent, busy housewife, rearing a family of five children; she also engaged in domestic tasks for more fortunate families, in order to augment our meagre housekeeping money. I was their fourth child, born in 1932. Grace and Joe raised five very grateful children in an atmosphere of love, sprinkled with laughter, tinkled with music. We were warm, never hungry, always wore clothing that was 'clean and well paid for'. What joy! The inheritance of good genes.

Grace and Joe determined that they would give their five children optimum opportunity to get 'a good education' and inculcated in their family the desirability of leading lives based on the strong tenets of faith, hope and charity. We all barracked for Richmond—the Tigers—which helped. At age 57, Joe had his first glass of beer. 'I always yearned for a glass of beer' he said, 'but my first priority was to raise my family'.

> We were warm, never hungry, always wore clothing that was 'clean and well paid for'. What joy!

Educated by the Sisters of Mercy, then the Christian Brothers, I left school in 1947 aged fifteen, worked as a 'bank johnny', went working on farms as a labourer; I had the year 1949 in Queensland working on a horse stud; next job was at a sheep station as 'cowboy/butcher'. I then headed for the Northern Territory. Seventy years onward, I am in Alice Springs, ever watchful, always positive, brimming with ideas. Seeking to understand this wonderful land.

I always stress that I am not talented in any capacity other than as an observer. I have travelled extensively around Australia and am always on the lookout for talented people and good ideas. I am not an engineer, not a scientist, not an economist, not even a good bushman in the real sense of the term. I am somewhat apolitical, but invariably vote for the person most likely to serve Australia commendably. I am aware of my strengths, I seek to acknowledge my weaknesses; I often rue the latter.

I inherited a great love of wordsmithing from my very talented father. I heed at all times the good advice given to me by my perceptive mother: 'Wherever you go in life, Teddy, keep sweet with the cook and be a good listener'. Great advice

Grace. I rabbit on occasionally, but when necessary I listen, ask questions galore, always watchful for the gems to come my way. My usual way of expressing myself is in the composition of songs. I have thirty albums of recorded songs, mostly my own 'words and music'—although I can't do 'dots on lines'. In recording the songs, I surround myself with expertise; it seems to work.

So I seek herewith to plot the course for a better understanding of Australia. There are monumental deficits to overcome in terms of economic revival; we need the bolstering of morale in all quarters. We need to treat one another better; specifically, all Australian males—and females—must be instructed in Ethics from day one. There is an urgent requirement for us to do sensible things to reduce climate change: we owe that to our children, for we have impaired their inheritance. The only approach to all of the above is mindful boldness, long term planning and maximum use of of our vast national resources by our wonderfully diverse population. We can change from being a manipulated, lesser nation to become a commendable, international dynamo.

> **So I seek herewith to plot the course for a better understanding of Australia.**

2 THE REPUBLIC

LET'S OPEN PROCEEDINGS WITH THE AUSTRALIAN REPUBLIC. In earlier times, I always resiled from discussions about the Republic; my stance was that we have more important things to do than pursuing divisive issues. I voted against the notion of a Republic in 1999, a loaded referendum cleverly framed by John Howard to ensure its downfall. 'If it ain't broken, don't fix it' was Howard's crude message. I felt that a Republic would eventually impose itself on us, with no realistic opposition. The old system is now broken irrevocably and we should seize the opportunity to effect a change. The end of Queen Elizabeth's reign as Queen of Australia would be a courteous date.

Professor Jenny Hocking's resolve to have the letters between Governor General John Kerr and Buckingham Palace released for public perusal provides proof that there was knowledge, if not collusion between the Queen, Her Personal Secretary Charteris and Prince Charles, to encourage the Governor General to effect his traitorous betrayal of Australia, when he sacked the Prime Minister legally elected by the people. The letter from Charteris to Kerr dated 25 October 1975 begins …

> Dear Governor General,
>
> Many thanks for your letter of 30th September which The Queen has read with the greatest interest. Her Majesty commands me to thank you very much for keeping her informed, through your letters, of developments in the present situation which raises so many difficult constitutional and political problems for you: or perhaps I should say "may raise" as we must all hope that in the event they may not arise …

Kerr sacked Whitlam on 11 November 1975, three weeks later. Professor Hocking perceptively points to the fact that neither the Queen nor her Secretary asked Kerr, at any stage: 'What does your Prime Minister think?'

A Republic is no longer a divisive issue: bring it on! I recommend readers to consult the various works of Professor Jenny Hocking and read the excellent book *Elect the Governor General*—David Solomon 1976.

But first, let's check out the rest of the world. There are few republics that are admirable, mainly because of seemingly inevitable corruption around the actual Presidency. It is fairly obvious that in Australia the Republican movement will only succeed if there is a democratic process, whereby *the people* have the opportunity to *elect* the President; that was revealed in the 1999 referendum vote. Never, say the purists: the President must be *appointed* by the Parliament, otherwise we will follow so many existing Republics, where tyrants or lesser beings are appointed on the basis of wealth, quest for power, political persuasion, race, religion or all of the above—all backgrounds shown to be dangerous.

> **A Republic is no longer a divisive issue: bring it on!**

What we need in Australia is an *amalgamation* of the two schools of thought, to achieve the best possible system.

I suggest that the position of President be defined as simply *Head of State,* no more no less, with the President living at Government House, Canberra—performing the familiar duties so dutifully achieved by all but one Governor General incumbent in 120 years of Federation—but responsible to, replaceable by, the people of Australia. I suggest a term of four years, followed by an election to allow a re-elected incumbent to seek an additional four years in office.

This largely follows the American pattern: the maximum Presidential term of eight years. The essential difference I propose is that the Parliament selects a panel of four candidates, chosen with a two-thirds majority of both Houses; the panel of four names is presented to the national electorate for preferential voting. No boring campaigns! The names and backgrounds of all nominees will be well-known to voters. The new President is sworn in by the previous President and then opens the first Parliamentary session of her or his Presidency.

> Of course there will be political *overtones*. Few if any successful people in life are totally apolitical.

Of course there will be political *overtones*. Few if any successful people in life are totally apolitical. But there are many eminent Australians capable of putting aside anything prejudicial in their private lives, in order to serve the entire nation to the best of her or his ability. We have received excellent service to date, with just one defaulter since the appointment of Governors General became the right of the Australian parliament, beginning with Sir Isaac Isaacs in 1931. But let the will of the majority prevail: power to the people, wherever possible.

How different then would Australia need to be as a Republic? Less is best I suggest. There would definitely be a requirement for a new Constitution. It will be the responsibility of the federal Parliament to provide the framework of firstly the Constitution, then the format of the new nation.

Presumably the will of the public will be to retain State boundaries. I support that, with a single suggestion for amendment. For reasons which I hope to present impressively in subsequent chapters, I propose a new state, to be titled *North Australia*, covering the mainland and all islands north of the Tropic of Capricorn (see map). This would be a salutary acknowledgement that the country north of that line is *sub-tropical*; it should be treated thus in respect of agriculture, horticulture, pastoral pursuits, fishing and marine farming. Its geographical position says that national defence headquarters, bodies engaged in maritime research and exploration, all international welfare organisations should be based in the north, with the stress on a positive rather than an aggressive presence. Our clarion call should be: We are here to help neighbours in need, whenever.

There would be the requirement to conduct a plebiscite among local residents to decide whether Rockhampton, Queensland—at present shown on maps as being located *on* the Tropic of Capricorn—would be included in North Australia or remain with Queensland. Alice Springs (NT)—where I live—is located 15 km south of the Tropic of Capricorn, but is geographically more connected to South Australia than the tropical north.

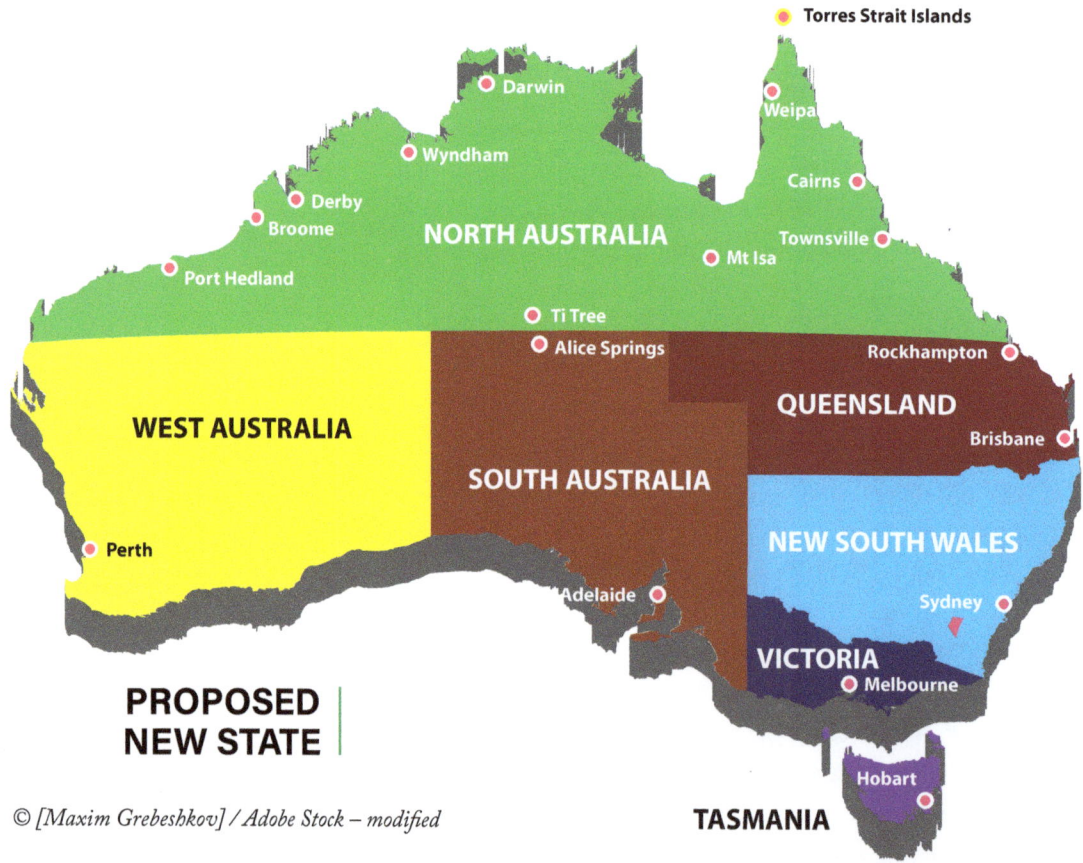

© [Maxim Grebeshkov] / Adobe Stock – modified

Mining is always and must continue to be on the social and political agenda in all regions. There should always be a policy of knowing what minerals we have at our disposal; more importantly, there must be long-term policies regarding our exploitation of those minerals. It is not good enough for us simply to be a quarry for other more industrious nations.

I am personally opposed to the mining of uranium, resolutely opposed to mindless, dangerous pursuits like fracking, for those endeavours take us on the dangerous path of guessing, rather than knowing what is good for us and indeed the world. Fukushima Daiichi and Chernobyl must always be the events to remind us that we are nowhere near ready for nuclear power. The frackers try to convince us that we need to access gases below the surface by explosions—perpetrated in a country that is 'water poor', very dependent on ground water! Not only do the sums of the frackers not add up; they know not what they do. The Great Artesian Basin should be declared an inviolable National Park. Leave the gas where it is: let's concentrate on renewable energy sources and look after Australia in the process. The frackers are motivated only by short-term greed. They say: fracking is OK 'in some areas'. They should be submitted to the NIMBY test.

Coal is coal: we have used it to a level of excess, but we did not know better. We now have irrefutable proof that coal use must be scaled down, ceased as soon as possible. We now suffer the consequences of the Industrial Revolution; our children lay the blame at our feet. Yet *The Australian Minerals Council* is cocky, adamant that we will be selling coal to other countries in fifty years time. The big powerbrokers are buying up old coal mines. Let us take some wind out of their sails. We can do better.

At the same time, it is crucial to know what minerals are below the surface, if only to enable us to insist that there is no mindless exploitation. Let us have sound, bipartisan policies that relate to all knowledge of minerals. Leave the "frozen" minerals where they are: they won't disappear.

But by all means let us have responsible mining of the necessary, available minerals.

3 New Regional Centres

The future of the new State of Northern Australia will be discussed in future chapters. What of the existing states, Tasmania, Victoria, South Australia; what of the reduced in area states of Western Australia and Queensland?

It will be good sense to retain the Australian Capital Territory in its present form, with a strong, elected ACT Legislative Assembly. The ACT will be the home of the President, the Prime Minister, the centre of federal (Republican) power. Most of the Northern Territory—the area north of the Tropic of Capricorn—would become part of the new state: Northern Australia.

I support the notion of amending existing State governments. Such a prospect would undoubtedly come under the consideration of the body appointed to create a new Republican Constitution. Revision, preferably termination of the 1901 Constitution, would be a positive move in any case.

The present Australian Constitution was the the product of the supposed wisdom of our 'Founding Fathers', a whiskery group of self-centred old white men, who selfishly, zealously set out to maintain the power they had established in the states that were formerly colonies of the penal settlement set up by the British in 1788. In the 1901 Constitution this group established state control over every meaningful function. They imposed on us an inflexible, written document that has impeded national development ever since.

In 1964, Donald Horne wrote his fine book *The Lucky Country*. The book was generally misunderstood, accepted by too many of us as an outline of how fortunate, how clever we were, inheriting the lifestyle established at Federation in 1901. Horne told us that yes, we were fortunate, in that we lived on an island continent in a temperate climate, but we were certainly not clever. What we had created was a mess, which in many respects is ongoing. We will only repair that ongoing governmental shambles at the point where we formulate a totally different national Constitution; let us drastically amend state governments and remove state control of national issues.

It is high time to discontinue the so-called Upper Houses still existent in most states. They are bastions of privilege, seemingly intent on delay and confusion. I guess the majority of voters would see sense in retaining scaled-down State governments and the inherent 'legal system' that has been established over many years. But the nation's *Essential Services*—the various Courts, police, fire, health and education and the personnel involved, would perform better with federal control and regional supervision, based on knowledge and understanding of the various *regions*.

I would opt for enhanced regional—nowadays called 'local'—government. Let's consider Victoria as an example. Regions surrounding towns like Ballarat, Bendigo, Geelong, Euroa, Wodonga and Sale are ranked as equals to a 'reduced in power' Melbourne region. A similar system of regional empowerment throughout the nation would inhibit the existing lunacy, whereby state capitals become bigger, over-populated and people are tempted to leave underprivileged country regions and move to the already over-crowded capital cities.

Sadly, only Hobart, Adelaide and Darwin remain at a desirable size among capital cities at the moment. We can't continue to create overpasses, dig tunnels and build skyscrapers even higher than at present: it borders on madness. But let us have passenger-friendly expressways, tunnels and highways linking all regions. Especially in North Australia, let's have bitumen roads—wider than at present—as a top priority.

The total question of sovereignty will also be discussed in chapters to follow—especially the sovereignty, however limited, available to First Australian nations. I suggest that all future migration issues be considered against the need to create sensible, workable, compatible regional centres, where local government runs the show on its terms, with federal (Republican) support and encouragement. Critics say to me: 'You can't stipulate where migrants will live!' I invariably respond with the pantomime phrase: 'Oh, yes I can!!!'

Established, definitely racial but not racist groups—like the Italians in North Queensland, the Greeks in Melbourne and Darwin, the 'Barossa Deutsch' in South Australia, the Chinese—and, more recently Vietnamese—in Darwin, have shown how to do it; they established long-term economic and cultural presence in their regions, through sheer hard work. They are unmatched as loyal Australians. I often describe them as 'more Ocker than Paul Hogan'. And who would deny First Australians the right to political cohesion in their own, established regions in the proposed new State of North Australia? Nationally, as merely 3 to 5% of the national population, they will confront difficulties, but it is much better for them in the north, where some level of cohesion is already strong because of their bigger numbers, pride in their culture, traditional knowledge and adaptability.

In Queensland there is general distrust of 'those bastards down south', indeed, north of Rockhampton that animus is directed at Brisbane! That would all be amended if my proposed state of North Australia and regional control therein eventuated. Joh Bjelke-Petersen, Premier in a gerrymandered Queensland (though born a Kiwi) had absolute contempt for the Australian Federal government. Tiger Brennan, the fiery Northern Territory politician,

> In Queensland there is general distrust of 'those bastards down south' ...

constantly railed against 'those blinking bods in Canberra'. WA Sandgropers bemoan 'the wise men from the East' and occasionally propose secession. We have had a history since Federation of distrust and wrangling between the Feds, the States and Territories, especially since the Federal government gained legal supremacy for collecting Income Tax and later established the Goods and Services Tax, thereby holding the financial power.

Despite opposition, the unique German leader Angela Merkel invited Syrian refugees in huge numbers; after a shaky start, her charitable act seems to have prevailed. While I am opposed to the oft-proposed notion of 50 million people in Australia, I think 30 million can be handled adequately as long as there is industrialisation of our north, discouragement of new citizens from living in the existing capital cities and creation of meaningful jobs for all residents of all regions.

> We have had a history since Federation of distrust and wrangling between the Feds, the States and Territories ...

What shall we call the President? Here is a wonderful opportunity for my proposed First Australian Academy—see Chapter 8—to come up with a suitable Australian title, applicable to both genders. *Maluka* and *Bunggawa* are appropriate NT titles known to the author, but I have only ever known these titles to be bestowed on males. The white man Aeneas Gunn was respected as *The Maluka* (emphasis on the first syllable) at Elsey Station by both blacks and whites. It has a good sound to it. *Mal*-oo-ka! All Australians are urged to read "We of the Never Never".

I suggest possible 'titles' not only to impress the reader with my knowledge(!) but also to demand the *correct* pronunciation of First Australian words. Please, let us stop using the word Makarrata—the white man's suggested name for a Treaty—but sounding, in current discussions, more like the name of an American gangster: Mack A'Rata. It's an inappropriate word in any case! See Chapters 11–14.

The Tiwi, renowned for gender equality, have the male word Arikulani and the female word Arikulanga as accepted terms for 'Elder'; Elders are revered, regardless, in a valid geruntocracy. But let's handball this and other heritage questions to the *Academy*—which, if I am correct, will have a proper Australian title—as it should. The Voice? That's what the Uluru Statement sought. A Voice? Easy: forget the referendum idea though.

The support for regional government that I propose, while still retaining the old State borders on a nostalgic level (who would dare discontinue State of Origin Rugby League matches? The Melbourne Cup? The Sheffield Shield?) would mean a similar membership of the House of Representatives, but what of the Senate? I say, let's keep the Senate.

If we were to return to the original 1901 concept that the Senate is a *States House of Review*; if we also retained the very effective American-style *Senate Committees*, I think we would create a Republic government capable of delivering the goods. But I think we should limit the Senate to six members per State and two for the ACT, giving a total membership of 44.

Elections for both Houses? The sooner we settle for same day elections for the Presidency, the House of Reps and the Senate, every four years on a prescribed date, the better. The present three year system is predictably self-centred, opportunistic, unimaginative and runs something like this:

- Year One: Let's celebrate: Jobs for the Boys! And a few Girls!!!
- Year Two: Plan for the pork barrelling that will please our supporters and prepare the path for
- Year Three: Hefty funding, especially in marginal electorates, to ensure victory at the opportune time chosen for the election.

The world screams for effective leadership: Australia has rarely known it. Even our best governments should have done it better.

Above: Flag A, *below:* flag B

4   The New Flag

As with the Republic, when the national flag was discussed previously, I did not participate, on the same grounds: divisive issues are best avoided. I am not strong on flags in any case. I have seen too many incidents where flag-waving has been so aggressive, so provocative. However the time is right to establish a new flag that relates only to Australia as a peace-seeking nation.

There have been suggestions about amending the existing flag by replacing the Union Jack on the present flag with the recognised Aboriginal flag and retaining the various stars. I certainly reject the suggestion on aesthetic grounds; but my principal objection is that only First Australians should have power over the use of their flag. It is a symbol that has prompted an admirable unity among them. It is theirs and theirs only. It is incumbent on the Australian nation—here is another role for the proposed First Australian Academy—to step into the present-day copyright nonsense involving licensing rights for the Aboriginal flag.

There is always contention around the present national flag—the Union Jack with the Southern Cross and the Commonwealth Star. It is quite attractive aesthetically but it is like reports about motor accidents: no two people think alike. Some claim that in various battles Australian participants carried the Blue Ensign, others say the Red Ensign, others insist that the actual British flag—the entire Union Jack—represented Australia.

It's all a bit silly really. The present flag is red, white and blue. Australia's *official* colours are green and gold. In *Pantone Colour Reference* the green is specified as 348C, the gold is 116C. The colours were officially declared by Governor General Sir Ninian Stephen, acting on the advice of Prime Minister Bob Hawke, on 19 April 1984.

Nobody queries our sporting uniforms, invariably green and gold.

Although Australians understandably identify with the *Constellation Crux*—the Southern Cross, the best known stars in Southern Hemisphere skies—there are other countries (especially our neighbours, New Zealand and Papua New Guinea) that also recognise it on their official flags.

I suggest either of these designs offered here (flag A or flag B) which would be exclusively Australian, in recognition of our newly acquired independence.

> It's all a bit silly really. The present flag is red, white and blue. Australia's *official* colours are green and gold.

5 The Economy Post-Covid

The Covid-19 Pandemic has decimated the world population; notwithstanding the medical issues confronting us, we witness unprecedented numbers of people thrust into the worst economic circumstances imaginable. Unemployed numbers surge; young couples with young families are desperate to pay mortgages or rent and retain the commodities considered 'normal' these days—cars, domestic appliances galore. They have the crucial task of caring for their young families, even required to supervise their student activities. Many helpless people are cashing in their superannuation entitlements, thereby jeopardising their retirement years. There is no bright light in sight and it may well be years before anything approaching normality is restored. Mental health is under constant scrutiny and is perhaps the greatest single concern for the future. Morale depends on a sound economy.

> The Covid-19 Pandemic has decimated the world population ...

Governments throughout the world are creating new fiscal terms on a daily basis as they access seemingly bottomless buckets of 'taxpayer dollars'. Cynics remind us that the same taxpayers will be required to repay the accrued debts over the next fifty or so years. Economic attitudes seem to differ from the old days. We are told that Richard Nixon declared that nations do not need to have gold ingots to substantiate their governmental wealth: just keep printing the banknotes. Ignoramuses like me hear economists talk of MMT (Modern Monetary Theory) as they seek to come to terms with the impossible.

One thing can be guaranteed: the rich will get richer, the poor will have to scale down their ambitions. Somehow or other, we will survive, hard as that is to believe. Already enterprising citizens are determined to develop solutions, especially at local level. We human beings are a very suspect species, yet when doom seems imminent Simpson appears with his donkey, somebody opens a soup kitchen, an envelope is popped into a letter box. Admirable stuff: may it continue.

In Australia there must be a national plan based on reality. In World War II, I recall that the nation packed food parcels to send to the UK; Australian Comforts Fund staff ensured that troops were sent essential commodities. Everybody—and I mean everybody—purchased War Savings Certificates and Bonds. I seem to remember buying War Savings Certificates @ 2/6 from my paperboy earnings.

There are many people in Australia who are millionaires and indeed quite a few who can access one billion dollars each in their own right. Good on them: in most cases they have worked hard, planned well, invested wisely. What better investment than our own country? They should be given tax incentives to invest in worthwhile national projects. Many of them skilfully avoid paying tax in any case. As Kerry Packer indicated, there is nothing wrong with minimising income taxation if done legally.

Superannuation is nowadays such a vital factor in our lives, thanks to Paul Keating. The billions of dollars in Super Funds should be invested wisely in projects that will benefit their owners, the delightful prospect being that the same people work on 'our national products' until it is time for

> One thing can be guaranteed: the rich will get richer, the poor will have to scale down their ambitions. Somehow or other, we will survive, hard as that is to believe.

dignified, comfortable retirement as a consequence of forethought. Let's revitalise trade unions to organise such things. Fortunately Greg Combet and others seem to have a good grip on requirements.

The federal government must put before the people a Five Year Plan, a Ten Year Plan, a Twenty Year Plan, a Fifty Year Plan. Let's indicate the stages whereby specific targets will be achieved within those time spans. In every consideration we are talking jobs and a more equitable distribution of wealth. Jobs ensure wages, wages are spent within our nation, creating more jobs, more business opportunities. Bob Hawke sought to do it: let's actually eliminate poverty and inequality.

A major concern will be jobs for our youth. I talk to young people and they are fearful of the future. Australian universities are popular, particularly for Asian students who take the opportunity to improve their English as they study their various tertiary courses. That is very beneficial for Australia, culturally and economically. There is understandable enthusiasm for IT study among Asians and that is shared by many Australians in the same age groups. But we can't all be computer wizards; there has to be a better future than 'lookin' at my phone' as Pete Denahy warns us.

Yes, we want IT specialists, doctors, dentists, engineers, nurses, pilots, lawyers, scientists, but not every young person has the IQ required for such levels of achievement. When I was a child in the 1940s the majority of boys went into apprenticeships/trades at what were called 'Tech Schools'. Girls in equivalent numbers attended 'Domestic Science' schools. I acknowledge that times have changed, but I can't help feeling that the 'apprenticeship' approach of those days is a sound method of pursuing any course for a young person, given the certainty of it all: a guaranteed job, the delight of achieving. Just change the names to 'Trade Schools' and forget the gender nonsense. The world will always need plumbers, cooks, hairdressers, mechanics. Boys and girls, line up!

In Chapter 6 I will propose voluntary, non-militaristic National Service for all Australians aged 18–20. Adequate remuneration must be a component. All proposed specific activities will be earners, not just for the individual youths, but for Australia itself. And what a morale booster for the young. Again—adulthood, here I come.

In Chapter 8 I will advance the notion of two Academies, one of them being the President's Academy, whereby a selected group of eminent, successful Australians will establish a Fifty Year Plan to provide guidelines for long-term bi-partisan planning and policies, binding *in principle* on future Republican/Federal governments, regardless of their political alignment. Let's establish the 'don't go there' principles. I'd start by banning cotton growing and fracking. They are both so wrong for Australia.

In Chapter 9 I will propose the industrialisation of the north, together with the long term project, The COOMBS/O'CONNOR Grid, to eliminate drought and reshape attitudes to inland Australia. That will require huge government and private investment for a long period; early in the piece it would need huge commitment of governmental support.

In Chapters 13 and 14 I will suggest ways in which First Australians can be assisted to become wealthy in their established Heritage Nations, a welcome change from today, where it is often assumed that they have nothing positive going for them.

We can create a better Australia.

We can create a better Australia.

6 NATIONAL SERVICE

NATIONAL SERVICE IS NOT NEW TO AUSTRALIA. MY TEENaged Dad was in 'the cadets' in 1914. I was never required to participate in national service, but I think I would have enjoyed it. Many countries prescribe it for their youth. But there is no doubt that the rigged 'lottery' created in Australia to provide soldiers for the Vietnam war created an uncompromising antagonism to compulsory National Service in the minds of most Australians. Many *Nashos* survived the Vietnam experience with dignity, despite being demeaned and deeply offended by the hostility they encountered for many years subsequently. Salute the heroes indeed.

A sizeable percentage of Australian voters would support the notion of acceptable National Service, but I want to remove any overtones of war. I advocate optional, non-militaristic duty as a prospect for all 18–20 year old Australians, regardless of gender, allowing our young people the opportunity of a guaranteed period of paid National Service doing constructive things for themselves, our nation and the world. I recommend a two year term of duty, with incentives like—again optional—six months in an overseas posting. I also suggest an optional opportunity to

> I advocate optional, non-militaristic duty as a prospect for all 18–20 year old Australians ...

spend six months of the two years in a language laboratory, learning at top level a language other than English. That type of course could be organised by the Department of Foreign Affairs. What an opportunity for First Australian and other *Nashos* to become fluent in Pitjantjara, perhaps during a productive stint in Central Australia? See Chapter 16.

Other options could offer twelve months in any of the three armed services, but not involved in anything aggressive. Or twelve months in any of the 'essential services'—police, firefighting, St John Ambulance, Volunteers Abroad, World Vision etc.

The admirable *Duke of Edinburgh Scheme* shows us that Australia has a wonderful opportunity to use our enthusiastic, joyful (for they are volunteers, remember) youth to best advantage. What a boon energetic young *Nashos* would be around Retirement Homes, First Australian Heritage Nation enterprises, Kibbutz-style operations that I will outline in my proposals for bush fire control. See Chapter 10.

> The admirable Duke of Edinburgh Scheme shows us that Australia has a wonderful opportunity to use our enthusiastic, joyful (for they are volunteers, remember) youth to best advantage.

Pay? Transport? Accommodation. All I suggest is that a sensible rate of pay be established—perhaps double the Newstart rate, plus incentives wherever possible? I feel that *Nashos* should be subsidised to travel on existing and newly created coach services within Australia, rather than by air; that they be given incentives to provide their own transport to their chosen destination. They thereby get to 'see' Australia better, to understand their fellow Australians, to have greater mobility in their free time. Accommodation in work situations must be provided at an appropriate level. The existing backpacker facilities are a fair guide: Aboriginal Hostels have resolved many tricky issues over the years.

This is the sort of task that some people are born to organise. Jacqui Lambie, Minister for National Service. All those in favour?

How many would apply to be *Nashos*? Who knows? It depends how exciting we make it. One would hope that around one million young Aussies would be interested at any given time?

I applaud the many schemes that bring Pacific Islanders and others to Australia for various harvests and fruit picking. The scheme is obviously of mutual benefit to the economy of those nations. I would not seek to diminish what is obviously a successful strategy; I feel sure, however, that there will never be enough people to do the total number of jobs effectively. This is where *Nashos* could augment their base rate of pay by volunteering to share the workload. Who says Australians won't do menial tasks? Wonderful social contacts could be organised. Other countries have organised festivals of music and dance to celebrate the harvests. Mango Melodies at Mataranka? Apples Acapella? Let's innovate.

> **I applaud the many schemes that bring Pacific Islanders and others to Australia for various harvests and fruit picking.**

Overseas destinies? Although I support a Republic, now that it is not a divisive issue, I advocate staying within the British Commonwealth of Nations. Rejoining it was one of Nelson Mandela's smarter moves. Given independence, there is no reason to reject the many advantages our mutual colonialism has wrought, so one can expect that great opportunities will prevail or are capable of being created in friendly Commonwealth nations. If we were to show the way, perhaps other countries, especially New Zealand and Canada will follow suit. They seem to rank as our favourite cousins. India and Pakistan have so many skills to teach the world, although we must not follow them in over-population!

The Commonwealth Games is a very happy get-together every four years, wherever. What an opportunity for our youth, either participating as athletes or as volunteers in various capacities.

Uniforms for Nashos? I'm easy, but I'll leave that question to the experts. As with flags, uniforms can be confronting, but some of our Olympic uniforms have been superb.

7 Australia: A World Force

Australia is indeed a fortunate country. As an island continent, one nation, blessed with temperate weather and not yet over-populated, we have unique status in the world. Nobody else can beat that: not even New Zealand, although their country deservedly enjoys a better international reputation.

We can be much better and my book seeks to promote enhancement of an already promising situation. We must first and foremost establish pride in the ongoing presence of our First Australian heritage. That requires for starters a brave President, a courageous federal Parliament and people who know our history and our pre-history. We are indeed blessed, yet there are crucial social areas requiring humility, acknowledgement and a determination never again to have discriminatory laws based on race.

It's perhaps a trivial matter, but the National Anthem is a place to start. Look at the demeanour of the French, or the Welsh, and latterly New Zealanders as they sing their impressive National Anthems. In Australia there is general disapproval of our existing National Anthem on the following grounds:

- Most people think that 'girt by sea' is a joke line;
- Many people don't like the second verse, on the grounds that great National Anthems neither have nor need a second verse;
- Many people object to the statement in Verse 2:
    - ø For those who've come across the sea,
      We've boundless plains to share …

So I suggest a better approach. Let's have an optional first verse in Pitjantjara (see Chapter 16) or, indeed, any approved traditional Australian language. New Zealand has enhanced its National Anthem in this fashion. Let's also go for an amended first verse in English and—importantly—no second verse.

I am aware that many people would like to suggest amendments to the existing Anthem. Here is my suggestion. A crucial component is 'keep it simple'. Here is my proposed amended version in total:

> Our home beneath the Southern Cross
> Is framed by peaceful sea
> Australia is the land we love
> We are strong and free
> Our First Australians share with us
> A heritage so rare
> In joyful strains, then, let us sing *or* With joyful voices let us sing
> Advance Australia fair
> In joyful strains, then, let us sing *or* With joyful voices let us sing
> Advance Australia Fair

We have in Australia people deriving from over a hundred different countries who lead distinctive, effective lives as Australians. The world considers that Australians are 'different'—they variously see us as quaint, occasionally admirable, sometimes boring, usually aggressive, regarded as colonial lapdogs, formerly to Britain, latterly to the United States. Unfortunately that colonial background has taken us to too many wars that need not/should not have been fought. A notable, indeed the only exception was World War II, when Australia justifiably joined forces with Britain, other British Commonwealth nations and the United States, to fight against aggressive madmen who sought to take over the entire universe.

Unless we take drastic preventative steps Australia is heading for trouble in our international relationships. The pervasive lust for power that seems to turn human beings into deplorable monsters is seemingly on the world agenda for the foreseeable future. No names no packdrill, but power is perverse and pervasive. Let us strive for real leadership.

> **Unless we take drastic preventative steps Australia is heading for trouble in our international relationships.**

I advocate a future where we trade on our uniqueness and present to the world a nation that has adapted all the better attributes developed in other recognised, successful countries—for example, Switzerland, New Zealand, Scandinavia, Iceland, Singapore. We should then recognise the skills and commendable attitudes deriving from our various ancestries. In my own case, I delight in relating to my Celtic heritage. We must also acknowledge the commendable achievements of two flawed countries, once enemies in our history: Japan and Germany. Nowadays they both play an admirable role in the world as peacekeepers. Above all, we must recognise the power-wielders of the present world and not get too close to any of them. They are all dangerous.

In order to stay aloof, we should concentrate on continuing to be around in times of international crisis. We already have much to be proud of. Our efforts have been recognised and appreciated by international neighbours in events like tsunamis, floods, fires and earthquakes. Long may it continue to happen thus, as a natural, instinctive consequence. Darwin Hospital, for example, has a superb medical team, ready and equipped either for the group to travel overseas or to provide mass emergency treatment in their own headquarters. Way to go.

We can do better. The voluntary National Service members proposed in Chapter 6 could provide strong young arms, helping hands and youthful enthusiasm wherever needed, in so many capacities. Our Police Forces, firefighters and medics in all fields must have international awareness in the training of their staff, in order to continue to answer the calls as required.

We have, in our midst, Australian citizens who are fluent speakers of the languages of countries likely to be in need of assistance, in Africa, the Middle East, the Pacific. There is not much in physical terms that the big countries of the world—China, India, Pakistan, Bangladesh, the United States, Japan, Taiwan, Cambodia, Thailand, Vietnam, Korea, Laos and the entire continent of Europe might ever want from us, other than our raw materials and foodstuffs, but national disasters and health situations can occur anywhere and need expertise. I had a wonderful cousin, 'Sandy' Brennan, a clearance diver in the Royal Australian Navy. Sandy became an expert at underwater welding. If ever there was an 'underwater' crisis in any country, it was highly likely that the Australian government would fly Sandy there. We are in a position to recognise such Sandys within our midst, have them prepared and available, so that, in times of crisis, we press the appropriate buttons effectively. Remember the Australian participation in the unforgettable 'caves rescue' in northern Thailand.

International bodies of consequence like the United Nations and the World Health Organisation deserve our support, both financially and through our many levels of expertise. Likewise the many worthy bodies providing succour to those in need. Tim Costello has shown the light for many years, as have so many other eminent Australians. Let us really empower them and their organisations.

Yes, I am aware that it is usual for Australia to be represented in emergency overseas situations (other than war) wearing military uniforms and being armed. I acknowledge that there is a security aspect at those times and it is probably the only way to handle certain happenings. I stress the need for exemplary training and careful choice of personnel in all such cases. It only takes one idiot to stuff up a memorable project.

8 Two Academies

I AM A GREAT BELIEVER IN LONG-TERM PLANNING. I ALSO approve of habit-forming practices requiring predictable, unwavering behaviour, especially to show loyalty. In quest of a better Australia, given the present opportunity to courteously create a Republic, I see the need for the creation of two Academies:

- The President's Academy
- The Academy of First Australians

I have suggested (Chapter 2) that the President be Head of State, elected by the total Electorate for a maximum term of eight years. I also recommend that the President's Academy consist of thirty eminent Australians—four per state plus two from ACT, two from NT– for a five year term of service, to provide a handy "overlap" around the prescribed Presidential term of four years.

The President's Academy to meet twice a year at Canberra and deliver a State of the Nation Report annually. Thereby they would slowly, surely impose a wise set of 'national conventions' to guide the parliamentary legislators in their deliberations. The long term aim: the will of the people to prevail. A real democracy.

Appointed? Elected? I'm easy. The President is Chair. The type of Academy member I envisage: Janet Holmes à Court, Michael Kirby, Pat Turner, Louise Sauvage, Kurt Fearnley, Tim Soutphommasane, Fiona Stanley, Dick Smith, Ita Buttrose, Rupert Myer, Lowitja O'Donoghue, Frank Brennan SJ, Cate Campbell … et al. We are talking class!

Likely Agenda Items for Appraisal by the President's Academy

- Health: Hospitals, training programs, future and long-term planning, Mental Health, Aged Care
- Education: Training of teachers, long term planning, annual appraisal
- The Economy: Present state: recommendations, especially long term
- Heritage: First Australian issues, all other matters
- The Arts: Adequate funding, long term overview
- Mining: Guidelines for future activities. Appraisal of export markets
- The Environment: Climate Change, Wildlife, National Parks, Fires, Floods
- Energy: Tide, Solar, Wind, other
- Agriculture: World markets, long-term National Planning
- Foreign Affairs: General overview
- National Morale: Social issues. Youth welfare. The Aged. The Disabled.
- Population: Migration issues, decentralisation. Demographic concerns.

The First Australian Academy

I am not a First Australian and I usually insist that they speak for themselves wherever possible. That is desirable, but as a friend and supporter I offer the advice that compromise is often beneficial. As an example, the Uluru Statement sought the following:

- Constitutional reform to empower First Australians
- A Constitutional First Nations Voice

- Makarrata (sic) Statement—a Treaty
- "We were first counted in 1967: in 2017 "We seek to be heard"
- 'Truth Telling'—an appraisal of Australia's colonial history.

The Statement has been given general (tokenistic I suggest) approval by many Australians, but I was not surprised when it was interpreted negatively by the federal government, by some very powerful critics (in predictable public forums) and dismissed savagely in some quarters.

I think that any referendum on First Australian issues, put to the people of Australia in the privacy of the ballot box, has minimal prospect of national approval, even if there is bi-partisan support in federal parliament—and that is not likely to occur in any case. The 1967 referendum victory was an absolute aberration, never likely to be repeated under the existing Constitution.

> I think that any referendum on First Australian issues, put to the people of Australia in the privacy of the ballot box, has minimal prospect of national approval …

The reader is invited to refer to my Chapter 12 to consider thoughts on misguided—also mispronounced—use of the word *makarrta* and treaties generally.

The establishment of an elected First Nations Academy would be a positive start, achievable immediately, as a consequence of the 'race clause' Section 51 (xxvi) amended in 1967 to enable the Commonwealth to make 'laws in respect of any race'. That was interpreted in 1967 and continues now, as the opportunity for the Commonwealth to pass *benign* laws in respect of First Australians. Yet some activists demand its deletion! This is the goose that lays the golden egg!

An Academy is a Voice, a national First Australian Voice. The structure of a First Australian Academy must of course be established via sincere consultation, followed by a highly-publicised election of delegates, according to the wishes of the voters in various Heritage Nations—see my proposals in Chapter 15. The Academy would have legislated authority, along the lines of L'Académie Française

The Charter of the Academy? All matters of heritage can

come under scrutiny and discussion. An annual State of the Nation report, as with the Presidential Academy, would enable realistic, achievable targets to be presented for the guidance of the federal parliament and Australian people generally. First Australian leaders should realise that 97% of the population will never concede actual legislative power to 3% of the population, other than by election from all levels of society. But the majority is prepared to listen to common sense.

Place names, orthography, school curricula, national monuments could all come under the scrutiny of The First Australian Academy.

9 Elimination of Drought

Here are the thoughts of a layman, seeking the means to *eliminate* drought in Australia. It will be hard to get my ideas past the sceptics, I acknowledge, but I have had a long life of 'observing' this vast land; I feel I am entitled to 'have a go'.

I am 89 years old. Every five years or so I am told that 'we are experiencing the worst drought in Australia's history'. The TV screens show us skeletons of dead beasts, with red dust blowing everywhere. Earnest farmers and their families say: 'It's the worst in living memory'. Hanrahan says: 'We'll all be rooned'.

> I am 89 years old. Every five years or so I am told that 'we are experiencing the worst drought in Australia's history.'

I watched, fascinated as a boy, as the Snowy Mountains Scheme turned rivers inland, creating electric power at the same time. I was aware of the wonderful migrant intake that accompanied that daring scheme; it transformed Australia. I knew also of the hydro-electric projects that were undertaken even earlier in the endowed state of Tasmania. I know of the Bradfield Scheme, proposed, supported by many but never really contemplated. I have read

Ion (Jack) Idriess's book, *The Great Boomerang*. I was a good mate of Ernie Bridge and often listened as that eloquent Sandgroper outlined the benefit of piping the Ord and Fitzroy rivers southwards. Drought and the means of harnessing water have always dominated the minds of all Australians, especially country dwellers.

The moment the most recent drought comes under scrutiny, the Nationals demand 'More dams' and the Greens say 'Over our dead bodies'. Although dams are crucial, nationally, there is no point in constructing new ones unless it is going to rain in the specific catchment region. And the biggest problem with dams is evaporation: big and deep is good. Small is Band-Aid.

There has never been a national plan to resolve the drought dilemma. Regardless of the challenging climate there are many thousands of farms and grazing properties in marginal—often arid—regions; for better or worse the people in those regions are determined to stay there. Fair enough, for Australia is crucial in the world's food bowl' stakes: our role needs to be enhanced, not diminished.

> There has never been a national plan to resolve the drought dilemma.

No doubt about it, the nation springs to attention in every major drought. 'Drought relief' areas are defined and generous loans/grants are quickly bestowed by various governments; there is a bi-partisan tradition of political support for farmers and graziers going back to the early 1800s. Billions of dollars are dispersed, but the droughts continue, indeed get worse. Most of us live in cities and towns, but Australians yearn for the rural nostalgia inspired by Henry Lawson, A B Paterson, Will Ogilvie, John O'Brien, Mary Gilmore, Steele Rudd, Judith Wright, Bruce Simpson, so people of all political persuasions support the notion of 'drought relief'.

Paradoxically, there is never any criticism of farmers and graziers seeking relief. There is no castigation of farmers who insist on growing unsuitable crops like cotton, demanding inordinate use of precious water. In the process once thriving rivers become trickles at best. Nobody reminds them of the many good seasons they enjoy. No vitriolic phrases like 'dole bludgers' are uttered. Government funding in the form of loans and grants is immediate and unquestioning. The Queen kicks in. Farmers and transport operators in 'non drought' areas load semi-trailers with thousands of bales of hay. Meat trays are raffled throughout Australia to raise funds; truckloads of essential items are sent bush, to save country families from embarrassment.

An important paradox is that, on the TV screens, the background to desperate farmers and their families shows the viewer live cattle and sheep in surprisingly good condition: they hardly look drought stricken. Obviously, breeding stock must be retained at their best if there is to be a post-drought restart. Property owners outlay their already reduced funds on grain and hay at huge cost, to keep breeders alive.

In the awareness that government financial aid to drought-stricken areas will continue at a huge level in the immediate future, I propose that any farmers/graziers in those regions who receive 'drought relief' must, thereafter, follow official procedures concerning their properties: (1) they must never exceed prescribed stocking figures; (2) they must establish a feed lot, capable of always feeding that designated number of animals at all times, in all circumstances; (3) they must pay for water used in the process. It seems to me appropriate to have the broad principles of Peter Andrews Natural Sequence Farming applied to all regions prone to drought, indeed all of Australia: contour ploughing, restore carbon in soil, prevent salination.

Guaranteed access to quality, reticulated water must be a component of any plan to eliminate drought.

So I also propose—very basically (see map)—that a 'ring main' is established in inland Australia, west of the Great Dividing Range, a pipeline to enable water to be available for any dry part of Australia that needs it, as and when the different needs arise.

Thereby, 'drought relief' is no longer an issue. What I propose is a huge, national scheme, probably taking 25 years to complete. Slowly but surely, comparable to the Snowy Mountains Scheme of the 1940/50s, costing immense taxpayer

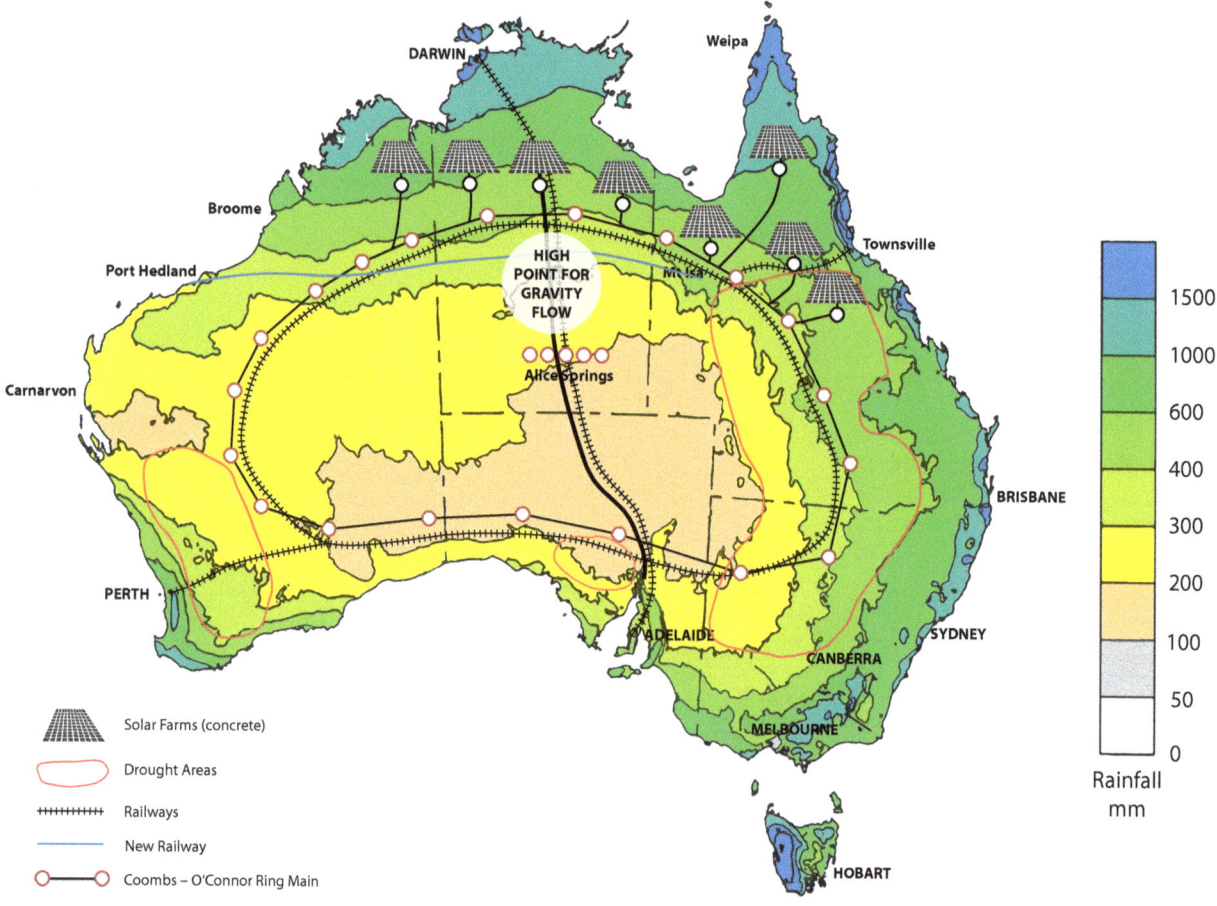

dollars, but also inviting private investment and, most importantly, creating millions of jobs. A project reminiscent of the mass employment schemes initiated in the 1930s Depression and the many government inspired projects undertaken as part of 'post war reconstruction'.

The national sums from all respects—mental, physical, economic, social—are worthy of the services of top actuaries, medical and financial wizards, adventurous agricultural and pastoral advisors. This requires national investment at the ultimate level. There are opportunities for regions themselves to be investors, as well as workers—and, thereby, become beneficiaries eventually. Create competition among regions.

It is the type of Keynesian economic project that would

hopefully attract individual, regional, and Federal support post Covid 19. Refill our national and state coffers by creating jobs and a prosperous future. Perhaps here is the unique political opportunity to create history: let's invite China and USA to become our partners in this massive project to "develop the world's food bowl"? What a coup!

China loves to 'think big'. At Cheng Du they have recently built the world's largest building, mainly concrete, steel and glass: its floor space would accommodate 300 MCGs. The Yanks are similarly gifted. A 'prototype' water tank called something like the 'FDR-MAO' would be a piece of cake. Various factors are relevant:

- huge rainfall from all appropriate quarters, but especially the tropical north, needs to be harnessed;
- harnessed water is channelled/piped into a huge network of water tanks, each the size of the MCG;
- at the same time, huge solar farms on concrete floors are installed with the major aim being (a) supply electric power wherever needed, but (b) also contribute—wherever feasible—to the catchment of water.

Thereby, there is at all times a massive volume of water available to be used wherever required, reticulated simultaneously—and at equivalent pressure—in Kalgoorlie (WA), at Mildura (Vic), Charleville (Qld), Ceduna (SA), Halls Creek (WA), or Mataranka (NT).

There are obviously huge engineering issues, where I have no knowledge. Stress on water tanks? Friction in piping of such huge amounts of water? Potability issues? We could have the experts as members of the President's Academy: let's pose the questions.

The reader will note from the map of Australia (opposite) that the proposed tanks are, wherever possible, in close proximity to existing railway lines. Well, this proposal is for a project even bigger than the Snowy Mountains Scheme which was the pillar of post war reconstruction in Australia after WWII.

Indeed, there will eventually be a total GRID—road, rail, water, electricity, with the consequent "industrialisation of the north". My suggestion is that the total project be titled *THE COOMBS O'CONNOR GRID*, after two great Australians: H C 'Nugget' Coombs, Director of Post War Construction in the late 1940s; and C Y O'Connor, designer of the Mundaring–Kalgoorlie pipeline WA.

Simultaneously, a new rail link connecting the Pilbara (iron ore) region of WA to the Bowen Basin (coal) of Queensland, via Mt Isa and Tennant Creek would connect all the required mineral deposits: iron ore, coal, silver, lead, zinc. That rail link has been proposed for many years by Shane Condon and his supporters, under the title *The Iron Boomerang*.

There would be, eventually, 100 or so huge tanks linked by the pipeline, with an accumulation of tanks around various regions, e.g., Alice Springs, (which is topographically high) to enable water to be 'gravity fed' wherever possible, as well as pumped from tank to tank as required in the total ring main system.

One of the ways of harnessing water—and simultaneously, generating renewable energy—is to build solar farms in heavy rainfall areas. Not only is the energy of the sun gathered, but, wherever it is deemed suitable, the solar panels are erected on

Below: Water tanks the size of the MCG, some elevated, some below ground level, dependent on topography. Connected by ring main.

© [pabloprat] / Adobe Stock

concrete floors at the standard 15° angle (see photo below). When it is fine, we merely harness the sun's rays. But when it rains, all the rainwater is collected and piped into one of the huge tanks (opposite page).

The sums are impressive. Take a place like Mossman Qld. The average rainfall is 100 inches a year. An old-fashioned 'inch' of rain is something like 25mm. If we construct at Mossman a concrete floor 5km x 5km on which we have thousands of solar panels, we capture 60 billion litres of water in a given year.

If we have a water tank the area size of the MCG—say 200 metres diameter and 100 metres high—it will hold 3 billion litres of water.

Yes, when it rains, there's not much solar energy to harness, but …

We construct solar farms near most tanks in any case. Occasionally, 5 inches of rain falls at Alice Springs. That is certainly worth catching, especially because in Alice we also have 300 + days of sunshine every year. All towns would welcome an additional huge tankful of potable water.

There are many additional and varied means of harnessing water into the ring main. Many rivers and dams attain

Below: Huge solar farms constructed on concrete floors, to enable harnessing of rain water when it falls.

© *[Blue Planet Studio] / Adobe Stock*

'overflow' status, sometimes to 'flood' levels—particularly the big northern rivers like the Fitzroy, Ord, Daly, Victoria, Katherine, Roper, Burdekin—not to mention the huge rivers of coastal New South Wales that often flood the landscape before they reach the ocean; floodwaters from such occurrences can be directed into the ring main, rather than spill into the sea. The Channel Country rivers of south-west Queensland take a 50 mile wide flow into Lake Eyre. Easy to divert some of that.

There are immense artesian and sub-artesian basins and aquifers available throughout Australia; let us not stuff up these priceless assets by mindless fracking! Storm water in all cities and towns is presently drained into underground pipes to avert flooding of streets and buildings. As a consequence of dry times, there has been massive investment on desalination plants. There are many dams, most of them subject to huge overflow in times of flooding. All of these sources must be considered for participation.

It is a delightful fact that rain falls in the north in the summer months; there is generally a dry summer in southern regions. In the south, rain usually happens in the winter months. Given this diversity, even the devastated Murray-Darling Basin could be topped up! Imagine?

Now for some lateral thinking! Alongside each huge prototype tank (each of which, of necessity, has a flimsy but effective lid, cf., gasometers) we place a smaller, open "overflow" tank, there for access by helicopters, which in the future will be the principal weapons in bushfire fighting. Dip! Fly! Access? Anywhere.

And let us not forget tourism. Tourists love train travel. The ring railway linking all the above facilities could cater for *The Train to Nowhere* to enable tourists to travel—endlessly if they wish! it happens on ocean liners—in luxurious trains, through the safest country in the world. Break the journey for a few days at the 6 Star Hotel between Kalgoorlie and Meekatharra. Regional talks? Cultural pursuits? Opera? Shakespeare? Golf? The world's largest golf course? What else is there to do? Nothing much. Swim in the pool. Watch the stars at night. Read your book. Think your thoughts. Relate to your loved one. All aboard!

10 BUSHFIRES

MY RECOLLECTION OF THE YEAR 1939 IS VERY VIVID. On 1 January 1939 I was introduced to my new brother Francis Geoffrey, later to be known as Tim. I had been taken to Ballarat for the day by my Uncle Jack and when we returned home to Coburg, suburban Melbourne, there was my Mum and this wonderful new brother!

A few weeks earlier, December 1938, my eldest sister Patricia (aged 16) saved—from her wages at Lincoln Mills—enough money to enable her to spend the Christmas fortnight at a 'Guest House' at Healesville, not far from Melbourne. She returned home, proudly showing us photos of herself, in her "joddies" (jodphurs), jacket, collar and tie, looking ever so flash, posed with the guests at this lovely big homestead with THE GLEN painted on its roof.

> ... *The Glen* was burnt to the ground in the dreadful fires that occurred on "Black Friday" 13 January 1939. Seventy one people died in those fires.

Two weeks later, *The Glen* was burnt to the ground in the dreadful fires that occurred on "Black Friday" 13 January 1939. Seventy one people died in those fires.

Since that time I have wept, over and over, as bushfires take their toll in fires that get larger, year by year, always accompanied by stories of huge losses of life, devastating pain, frustration and a national sense of ineptitude, despite the heroism of the huge number of firefighters—many of them volunteers—who gather from all around Australia and other worthy countries. It seems that Nature has forsaken us yet again; with climate change caused by we humans, we must accept that it will get worse. Things will only get better if we seek to understand our country, our world. We are not in charge.

We have Royal Commissions, we pin medals on brave persons, we mourn the agonising loss of so many of our citizens. I cannot imagine anything worse than being burnt to death in an Australian bushfire.

The perennial question asked is: 'Can we handle things any better?' Given that Australia is always required to consider bushfires, it would be incumbent on the President's Academy to ask this question incessantly.

People invariably suggest that the First Australians handled the country better in days gone by. Of course they did. They understood Nature; they travelled appropriately at the appropriate times, because the song cycles told them what to do, where and when to do it. It was relatively straightforward. Crucially, there were no fences. Wildlife, often even more alert than the very knowledgeable humans, took whatever steps or flights necessary to avoid coming to harm. Often both humans and wildlife then took advantage of the aftermath of the fires.

We are indeed fortunate that there are still many First Australians who understand Nature: we must seek them out, learn from them.

Western society changed things drastically. People demanded the right to fence land and build substantial houses and other buildings inside those fenced areas. So wildlife is confronted by human built barriers. Many settlers, demanding the joy of living in forest areas, failed—and still fail—to acquire the knowledge necessary to provide optimum safety. All would be well advised to listen to Chad Morgan, who sings: 'It's a dangerous game I'm playing'; I cannot imagine anything more dangerous than living anywhere near an Australian eucalypt forest.

Eucalypt forests are marvellous in so many respects and—in Australia generally—an invaluable asset. Eucalypt forests are safeguarded by our extensive declaration of National Parks: 75% of Australian forests contain almost exclusively eucalypts. The use of the timber and oils can thereby be controlled and there is the national benefit that the trees absorb carbon dioxide. They provide wonderful homes for wildlife and birds. Let's retain those National Parks and effectively create firebreaks within them. Not that we will ever eliminate fire. There are arsonists and idiots who boost their miserable egos by lighting dangerous fires, but the vast majority of bushfires are caused initially by lightning; thereafter the slightest breeze can become a menace.

Eucalypts are tall, often magnificently so. And that is a major worry, for in times of unheralded fire, the oils, gases and high foliage create fireballs that can traverse hundreds of metres in minutes, wherever the wind decrees. Thousands of hectares can be devastated in a day. That is bad enough in itself, but what of the precious wildlife, scurrying for their survival, but nowadays encountering fences and other blockades?

We see the residents of Malacoota standing in the ocean, helplessly awaiting their destiny. We bleed for the residents of so many other threatened towns, assembled on their football grounds; they know the might of forest fires.

I think that, generally, we should counsel people not to live in forest areas. Many will still insist: I have the right, they say. Good luck to them. But they will need more than luck. I have some suggestions.

As with other proposals in this book, I recommend concentration on one or two places for a start, to test a *different* approach. I try not to teach grandmothers how to suck eggs; I can't do it myself in the first place. But each summer, as I agonise, watching the predictable outcome of the now seemingly inevitable, predictable fires, I keep thinking: 'There's got to be a better way'.

Why not select a couple of typical Australian towns, set

in known fire areas? I have a couple in mind, but I do not have specific, detailed knowledge. I base my suggestions on what I hope is accepted as common sense. How about the total elimination of eucalypt trees in a sensible firebreak around the town, one kilometre wide? Bring in the bulldozers, the excavators, the topsoil. Create a garden bed that surrounds the town's houses and ancillary buildings.

> How about the total elimination of eucalypt trees in a sensible firebreak around the town, one kilometre wide?

I do not propose an arbitrary firebreak. Let local knowledge prevail; of course we do not obliterate assets like a koala foodline: we should be planting eucalypts for that requirement and prohibiting houses in such regions. There are many relevant factors like prevailing winds, the flow of creeks and rivers that will be known to experienced locals. But what must be created is the means of preventing an overhead fire from devastating an established town.

Having applied local common sense, there is now a cleared, sacrosanct strip one kilometre wide, available for locals to do sensible things on a communal level e.g., planting

Google Imagery ©2021 CNES/ Airbus, Maxar Technologies, Map data ©2021

deciduous European or Canadian trees that are often marketable in terms of timber; they are also very attractive, with their autumn tints. There can be commercial avenues of grape vines, plus non-flammable fruit trees—citrus, olives, almonds, dates, apples, pears, avocados, peaches, apricots, plums, nectarines. Let's not forget to plant, wherever possible, the inimitable Aussie natives—quandong, macadamia and the almighty *Gubinge*—the Kimberley version of the Kakadu Plum, the most concentrated source of Vitamin C in the world and, importantly, not a eucalypt. This 'firebreak strip' can become the 'funder' to support local sports teams, schools, hospitals, public libraries, whatever, from the earnings.

There will still be fires, so we must find the best means of controlling them. Let us first of all devise the best methods of prevention—sensible fire breaks in National Parks; patch burning by experts at the appropriate times; quality graded roads, especially to allow access to sufficient available water; the availability of graders in the summer months; the permanent involvement of skilled rangers.

> **There will still be fires, so we must find the best means of controlling them.**

The best form of containing fires is extinguishment. Local groups of firefighters are truly admirable already, but they must at all times be funded appropriately, provided with the best possible equipment. Best quality fire trucks must be available in abundance.

In Stuart Rees's recent book 'Cruelty or Humanity' and SBSs 'Dateline' program, it was revealed that Australia's sales of military equipment—orchestrated by the Defence Department—in financial year 2019–20 totalled $5 billion, more than our total earnings from export of wheat, wool (and wine) in the same period. I am ashamed of my country.

We embark on nonsensical projects like nuclear-powered submarines that are likely to be obsolete when delivered in fifty years time, rather than concentrating on essential fire fighting facilities, ground vehicles, aeroplanes and helicopters.

We must have the best possible communications facilities: in this era of computers and mobile phones, we need panels of trained people in centres—like NASA (USA) at times of satellite launches—looking at CCTV screens, doing the sums, co-ordinating movements of firefighting teams.

We will always have people who insist on living in such regions. They should be encouraged to build sensible houses. Forget the timber, folks. Steel or aluminium frames, CGI roofs, brick or rammed earth walls, rainwater tanks, swimming pools with pumps for fire control; eucalypt trees only in isolation; minimal fencing; mini firebreaks as above, with fruit trees, grapevines, colourful deciduous trees from other countries, keep the grass mown and green around the houses.

All sensible towns will have local consultative committees. Schoolchildren should at all times be taught the fundamentals, the discipline of living in such dangerous areas—use of pumps, chainsaws etc; how to drive appropriate vehicles; tidy habits, especially around roof gutters and outbuildings; care of domestic animals and wildlife; first aid training for treatment of humans and all animals.

The latest techniques in fire fighting must be known in all regions; governments and shires must fund adequate training and leadership. In recent years there has been increasing use of aircraft and helicopters, especially where the terrain is difficult. We must have the best machines and we must make available the cleverest sources of water. In Chapter 9 I recommended the creation of a prototype water tank, the size of the MCG, to be incorporated into the COOMBS/O'CONNOR GRID. Such tanks would be invaluable around specific towns, for general use at all times, with smaller overflow tanks available for helicopters to dip, fill, keep returning, in the event of local fires. Such a volume of water would also be there for firefighting crews with conventional fire brigade vehicles.

11 Cars and Car Parks

Who knows what Australia will be like in fifty years time? It seems that, if one can imagine something, there is a good chance it will eventuate. On a daily basis I marvel at the changes to my country—and the world—in my lifetime. We think of things like international travel, space exploration, computers, the internet, but it is good to reflect that the paint roller was invented in my lifetime!

There seems little doubt that in the near future pedestrians will wear an electronic panel: press button A and we go upwards, press button B and we go forward to various heights as required.

One other thing is for sure. For the next fifty years the majority of Australian people will still be driving motor cars, needing to park them while we go about our business. Hopefully, most motor vehicles will somehow run on electric power, the requisite energy harnessed and recharged within the vehicle itself. Great! But the vehicles will still require parking space.

> For the next fifty years the majority of Australian people will still be driving motor cars, needing to park them while we go about our business.

My wife and I were in England in the late 1990s. Middle of winter, pouring rain. A relatively small town. Every allotted parking space in town was taken. On the edge of town—one kilometer from where we needed to be—we found a space that enabled us to barely squeeze our car in. Then the long walk in the rain.

I spent the next week toying with the thought: There's got to be a better way.

I have watched the development of dairy farms since my childhood. The cows walk on to a large round platform, capable of rotation. The machines are applied, the cows are milked as the platform revolves, the cows are released. In my week of thought I developed a plan for a multi story circular car park, along similar lines. I did not 'invent' anything in the process and I now realise that similar principles have prompted the creation of such parks, especially in Europe, where 'space is always a precious factor in life, where there has been an admirable separation of town and country. Busy town, suddenly pleasant countryside.

Yes, we have plenty of empty space in Australia, but we need to be much more clever in the creation of our carparks.

Round PALIS Automated carpark, Germany. © palis.de

A particular problem is caused by people who wish to park for a lengthy period, while they are at work, at the theatre, dining out, wherever, whatever.

I advocate a multi-storeyed, circular structure with, on every level, an inside track that revolves. A patron approaches the venue at ground level and parks the car on a movable platform. The driver locks the car and goes to the desk to record arrival. The driver is allocated a reference number, describing where the car will be parked. Let's say Level 10, Bay 27.

Yes, we have plenty of empty space in Australia, but we need to be much more clever in the creation of our carparks.

The car is then moved forward electronically on its platform, as far as the revolving inside track, whence it is taken—still on its platform—to an elevator, to level 10. On the revolving inside track level 10, the revolving track takes the car to to Bay 27, where it is lodged in a space one metre wider and one metre longer than the vehicle itself.

When the driver returns to collect the car, the costs are paid, the procedure is reversed; the driver collects the car and drives off. Yes, that all takes time, but next time you park the car, check the watch, from go to whoa.

The space sums are worth doing. In the present ground level car parks around shopping centres, sufficient space has to be allocated in order to allow cars to be reversed, then driven off. Each car requires four spaces.

Let's go higher, automatically, reach for the sky.

12 THE FIRST AUSTRALIANS

THE PRESENT (OFFICIAL) DEFINITION—ACCEPTED THROUGHOUT Australia—is that a person is an Aboriginal or Torres Strait Islander if he or she *is* of Aboriginal or Torres Strait Islands descent and *is accepted as such* by other Aboriginals and Torres Strait Islanders.

Basically the only criterion is self-identification, indicating an entitlement to inheritance dating back to 1787. There are no tests (to date) although, for various reasons, some groups call for DNA evidence and certification. Various corporations in Tasmania already issue *Confirmation of Aboriginality Certificates* to approved members.

'Aboriginals and Torres Strait Islanders' is quite a mouthful, so I submit that the same outcome is achieved if people in those categories are known, exclusively, collectively, officially, as 'First Australians'. Essentially, the connective date is the year 1787, which means, bluntly, that they—through their ancestors—were here first, before Governor Phillip arrived in 1788.

All other residents of Australia may be referred to as 'Australians', if it is established that they *are*, by various means, Australian citizens.

My granddaughter—Jessica Egan—is a proud First Australian. I—Ted Egan, Jessica's grandfather—born in Australia in 1932, am proud to be an Australian, on the basis of my birth here. I am thrilled to have a genetic link to my more privileged granddaughter: we have many spirited discussions! Jessica's parents are my daughter Jacki and Malcolm, her First Australian father. Jess is our family's *prima inter pares*.

There is no traditional common noun to enable all First Australians to identify as members of a united race. There are many regional identifiers, but care and respect must be exercised. Victorians and southern New South Wales people refer to themselves as Kooris. Northern New South Wales people and southern Queenslanders call themselves Murris. Western Australia has many regional terms, principally Noongars in the southern regions. Southern South Australians identify as Nangas. Further north they are Anangu.

There are problems. In Arnhem Land, where the common identity noun is Yolngu, the word mari (sounds like Murri) means 'trouble'. In the Northern Territory nanga usually equals 'Asian'. Tiwi once identified themselves as Tunuwui, as distinct from Muruntawi (white people) and Monari (people of mixed race) but in recent years the noun Tunuwui is unpopular, interpreted as 'black'! An old—very black—Tiwi friend recently admonished me, when I used that word in conversation: 'Don't call us black' he said. Nowadays they refer to themselves as Tiwi, a word—like Yolngu—that simply equals 'we humans', to distinguish them from the many living creatures that share their extremely complex culture. Old Tiwi people often told me that the only noun to describe all of them was Ngeningatingauila. That old collective noun is seldom heard but is still understood; Tiwi is considered to be a more clever name. But it is exclusive. Very!

> I submit that it's not about skin colour: it's about identity and—in respect of Australia—rights of inheritance.

I submit that it's not about skin colour: it's about identity and—in respect of Australia—rights of inheritance. I propose that, in all official debate, we concentrate on using 'First Australian' as the means of identifying First Australian people and causes. Collectively they have the right to national recognition, based on inheritance. In my opinion First Australians is a more expansive, more dignified, more appropriate term than any other in current use.

Indeed I advocate the establishment of a National Register of First Australians, where First Australians themselves detail and maintain the inheritance details of all members. Such an archive would be extremely useful for procedures like *per capita* records, funding, elections to bodies like The First Australian Academy (see Chapter 8) and provision of accurate national statistics. The unification introduced when the Aboriginal flag and colours came into use was admirable; a Register would establish similar levels of pride, identification and recognition. Small honorific badges (cf. The Order of Australia) may appeal?

There are undoubtedly many First Australians who would object to this form of acknowledgement on principle. 'Here go the gubbas with The Stud Book again!' I argue that a National Register is the best possible way to unite under one flag, to secure optimum recognition and respect. I would not seek to make enrolment compulsory, as the self-identification factor is an adequate starting point. First Australians don't have to identify, but there is good reason for best possible numbers: per capita recognition and funding will be undoubtedly the way to go in most situations.

There are many contentious words in use: let me discuss them.

One constantly hears the word 'indigenous' and I am occasionally amused by 'indigenity' and 'indigeneity'.

The dictionary tells us that indigenous (adj.) is used to describe people and things 'originating in and characterising a particular region or country'. Pauline Hanson, Andrew Bolt and many other people insist that they are 'indigenous' Australians, on the grounds that they were born here. Good luck to them. Aboriginals of various skin tones claim the word as exclusive to them. Good luck to them too. But I argue that a person, animal or plant can not be '*part*-indigenous'. A coolibah tree is indigenous. Roses are red, but they are not True Blue Australian, not indigenous. Kangaroos, emus and koalas are indigenous. Camels should have been but aren't. Almost certainly Vincent Lingiari, Albert Namatjira and Truganini were 'indigenous Australians' in the true sense, being of full descent.

There are probably 20,000 people in Australia who, today, could accurately be classed as indigenous—once referred to as 'full bloods'. But that takes us into the *apartheid*-ish nonsense of percentages, checking nipples(!), splitting hairs and counting drops of blood. Nowadays one hears many people in Australia describing themselves as 'indigenous'—indicating that they are 'of a non-Caucasian skin colour'. As well as First Australian people of mixed descent, I hear Polynesian Australians, African Australians, Asian Australians, whatever, now using the word 'indigenous'—even 'black'—to describe themselves, occasionally with the assertion that they thereby deserve special treatment. Forget it. Greeks are indigenous to Greece. The Welsh are indigenous to Britain. That does not give Greek or Welsh migrants special status in Australia. Nor should the colour of anybody's skin. The principal issue is inheritance, genetic connection to Australia in 1787.

Even the words 'Aboriginal', 'aboriginal' and 'aborigine' are likely to confuse matters nowadays if we seek to talk positively about social progress in Australia. Of course it is fair and accurate to say that Aboriginals (with a capital 'A') are Australia's aborigines (with a lower case 'a')—the country's original people. But the overwhelming majority of today's First Australians are of mixed descent. They have every right to assert proudly their Aboriginality, their honoured status as First Australians; but rather than 'over-identify' as so many people do today, they are invited to also acknowledge other components of their DNA and behave accordingly.

I urge all First Australians of mixed descent to see Troy Cassar-Daly's program in the series *Who Do You Think You Are?* The famous Country Music singer relentlessly traced his dual Maltese-First Australian heritage with equivalent, admirable pride. In the Top End of the Northern Territory there is a huge extended family named McGinness that derives from the marriage of Khungarakung woman Alyandabu to the Irishman Steve McGinness. Leaders in Top End society, they proudly acknowledge their dual heritage. Indeed, on the basis of the sound dual education given by their parents, the five original children were leaders in the fight for 'Aboriginal rights' long before it became fashionable.

The famous First Australian John Moriarty identifies with his dual heritage. He was born at Borroloola NT to a tribal Aboriginal mother and an Irish father. John Moriarty played soccer for Australia: his First Australian daughter represented Ireland at tennis. What joy they have given to both nations!

Let's think again around divisive terms like 'Invasion Day'. Yes, 26 January 1788 can be recorded as the date of an invasion of 'somebody else's land'. But many of today's protesters inherited most of their genes from the same 'invaders'. Let's establish and honour a day we all proudly recognise as Australia Day. More of that later.

We used to hear reference to 'part-Aborigines' and 'part-coloured' people. Smart people sorted that out: 'Show me where my coloured part starts and finishes', my dear old mate Joe (Pamarai) McGinness (above) used to say.

In this debate, I am reminded of a somewhat gauche TV interview by Steve Vizard, when Whoopi Goldberg visited Melbourne. He opened with: 'So what's an important black woman like you doing in Australia?' Whoopi gave him a perceptive look and asked: 'Am I black, Steve?'

I hear more and more the inappropriate American phrase 'people of colour'. We are all people of colour. I am pinkish, spotted. The obvious, delightful fact about Barack Obama that the world, sadly, failed to recognise was that he was brown—half black, half white—a man for all seasons and situations and a colossal bloke in the process. We could have put paid to all the stupid race debates that plague the world if we had used him as a basis of recognition. He was a worthy man: why refer to him as the first black President? Or the first African-American President? Happy birthday, Mr President.

First Australians especially will be well-advised to tread

carefully in 'black/white' issues that often originate in the United States and then are repeated/modified around the world. 'Black' issues in the United States and elsewhere relate to descendants of former African slaves now seeking justice. That is a struggle that needs to be maintained—hopefully peacefully—but has little relevance to the Australian cause of justice for First Australians. The dispossession of the aborigines of North and South America does have relevance to Australia, but comparisons are rare. More's the pity.

I don't support the requirement for sporting teams to 'take a knee'. For one thing, I have had two knee reconstructions and cannot kneel without a cushion. But it's a stupid expression, rightfully satirised by Tom Lehrer in his song: 'Genuflect, Genuflect'. And it does not *prove* anything. It's not dissimilar to the linking of arms and pledging of pledges by men in 'no more domestic violence' campaigns. Duplicitous males are devious wretches: given appropriate caps to wear, they will put on an impressive display. But statistics tell us that far too many men believe they have the right to 'discipline' their wives and partners.

There are indications throughout the world that, henceforth, people classified as 'whites' will be held to account for the Middle Ages Crusades, all forms of colonialism, anti-Islam attitudes, slavery, exploitation and the taking of 'black' lives. Protest movements and demonstrations relating to those issues inevitably attract the participation of activists—mostly sincere—but also mindless Rent-a-Mob wankers. Of course people have the right to assemble. Of course the question of police brutality, indeed any form of racial persecution or discrimination, needs to be identified and remedied. Of course prejudice of any kind must be replaced by the inflexible stance that all people are born equal. Let true justice prevail. In respect of First Australians, a particular concern is to seek measures to ensure safety of all persons in penal custody: the Royal Commission on Aboriginal Deaths in Custody set out positive routines for prison staff, which must be implemented and maintained for all prisoners at all times.

The major problem that confronts First Australians,

however, creating their present underprivileged status, is not so much the colour of their skins (although that *is* often a factor); it is the shameful, legalised dispossession of their ancestors post-1788, followed by subsequent discriminatory laws, exploitative miscegenation and demoralisation.

In the United States, the major, disputed racial issues are based on a history where privileged white society—comprised of organised groups of migrants from Europe—first dispossessed the original inhabitants, the First Americans, in concerted campaigns similar to those used in Australia. Refugees and settlers with 'white' skins were encouraged to migrate from Europe and establish 'the land of the free and the home of the brave'.

> **The major problem that confronts First Australians ... is the shameful, legalised dispossession of their ancestors post-1788, followed by subsequent discriminatory laws, exploitative miscegenation and demoralisation.**

They then brought millions of slaves from Africa to bolster their affluent lifestyle. The African slaves had recognisable black skins; society was immediately divided into attitudes of superiority and inferiority; ongoing issues developed—based on 'blacks' versus 'whites'. It is said that 'the Devil will quote Scripture'. The white Americans justified their attitudes to the black slaves, by quoting Joshua 9:21–23, deeming them 'hewers of wood and drawers of water'.

The blacks are today referred to as 'African Americans': the whites are, by and large, Caucasians—'Americans'—with a European heritage. A civil war was fought. Thousands were killed; the slaves were granted freedom of sorts, but prejudices often became stronger thereafter, reinforced by legislation and sanctioned atrocities. For over two hundred years the United States has sought to impose positive change, but nothing seems to improve.

In the middle of the segregation are the mixed races—the 'Hispanics'; it is a surprise to find how much Spanish is spoken in the United States. The 'First Nations' people of both North and South America are largely overlooked, although some treaties have created security over 'reservations'.

I toured Australia in 1974 as 'support artist' for the wonderful singer Charley Pride, who refused to be drawn into racial debates. He said to me one day: 'People always want to identify me; I get called a Negro, an African American, often a nigger, but hell, man, I just want to be Charley Pride'. It was a joy to be in the company of Charley and his wonderful wife Rozene. Valé, old mate. Covid put paid to an admirable life.

There are elites in both black and white camps in the USA. The black achievers—Charley is a good example—have emerged at top level as film stars, in business, government, law, science, cultural pursuits—especially music and sport—accruing immense wealth and enviable lifestyles. They have not escaped discrimination; indeed, in some cases there seems to be a national determination to expunge some names from history. While people like "Sugar Ray" Robinson and other black boxers, basketballers, football stars and the odd solo singer like Nat 'King' Cole are revered, most Americans know nothing of Paul Robeson, renowned singer and activist—and, arguably, the greatest all round athlete ever produced in the USA. But Americans hate 'Communism' as they interpret the term. McCarthyism is alive and well.

Very few of the magnificent black female singers get the level of recognition they deserve. I acknowledge that many of them, stars like Sara Vaughan, Ella Fitzgerald, Nina Simone, Lena Horne were just so talented that the world applauded them, but at the same time they were victimised appallingly in their own country. Dorothy Dandridge once demanded her right to swim in the pool of the famous hotel where she had been engaged to sing. The pool was drained as soon as she vacated it!

The majority of USA people from all backgrounds are poorer, less talented, more aware of one another's shortcomings and attitudes. Conflict is often the outcome. The country has no health or social welfare policies covering all citizens. Citizens without monetary wealth are in jeopardy at all times. The attitude of police forces is constantly criticised, sometimes condemned. Drug and alcohol addiction is rampant. Lunatic gun laws are not only tolerated; possession of firearms is held to be a 'constitutional right': thereby mass shootings are commonplace. Absolute madness.

The United States is nothing like Australia. The regrettable events of the past, in our country, must be addressed, soon. Only we can achieve this. I consider 'Proper Justice for First Australians' to be the major social issue confronting our nation. The prime weapon for First Australians is not the colour of their skins, but their right to a proper inheritance, based on undeniable genetic links to their land-owning ancestors. A stark reality for them, however, is that they are 3% of the population, trying to convince 97% of other Australians that they deserve justice. They lack cohesion and power; they have no private source of funding. They lack political savvy. Despite many claims to 'fluency in our traditional languages', I know of only a handful of First Australian scholars competent to address the nation in both a traditional Australian language and English. Politicians from all parties offer insincere tokenistic support, but are rarely forthcoming. They know the old political maxim: 'There are no votes in blackfellas'.

There are now many other Australians with skins blacker than most First Australians; it would be tragic if justifiable First Australian causes were diminished thereby. There is a risk that First Australians—most of whom *don't* have black skins—will yet again be shuffled to the rear end of the queue.

Despite all the adversities wrought on them, the tolerance of the vast majority of First Australians is just so impressive. Over countless centuries they worked out how to understand this unique land; they pay tribute to Nature in meaningful songs and ceremonies; thereby Nature will provide. They are not farmers as we are occasionally led to believe, but they have 'the knowledge'; there is no environmental question unresolved in their thinking. They know they must live with their land, not try to conquer it. Over centuries, they organised dynamic kinship practices in respect of avoidance and marriage partners—procedures to prevent inbreeding that the nations of 'civilised' Europe required, but did not develop.

I wish that every Australian could share the joyful experiences allowed to me in my youthful years. Because I was the

> **The prime weapon for First Australians is not the colour of their skins, but their right to a proper inheritance, based on undeniable genetic links to their land-owning ancestors.**

beneficiary of a strong Western education I was employed by the Commonwealth Government in the Native Affairs Branch, listed in the Government Gazette in 1953 as a *Protector of Aborigines*: my mother was ever so proud. In reality, it was I who needed 'protection'; fortunately, my First Australian mentors were there for me at all times, in all things. Much laughter surrounded my inadequacies.

Around the above semantic quibbles, I recommend that the Prime Minister of Australia take the 'First Australian Affairs' portfolio and commence discussions on a reasonable basis with reasonable First Australian people: *we might be pleasantly surprised at the immediate effect on national morale.*

The reader should be told that in the 1950s I worked for the Native Affairs Branch of Northern Territory Administration. It was common at that time for Aboriginal people of full descent to be called 'natives'; there was shameful counting of drops of blood to create pejorative terms like half-caste, quadroon and octoroon. I feel terribly sad about that: we muruntawi (whitefellas) certainly had better opportunities. But in 1974 I resigned, to make way for the many young First Australian people that I had helped train to be the rightful advocates for a better deal for their people. Bring it on!

It was common at that time for Aboriginal people of full descent to be called 'natives'; there was shameful counting of drops of blood to create pejorative terms like half-caste, quadroon and octoroon.

13 Mutual Recognition

There is constant debate about Aboriginal Affairs. The nation looks for positive ways to 'close the gap'. As we should, for it is not a gap: it is a chasm. We need to be thinking big, encourage meaningful interpretation of our history and go back centuries in our reflection.

I hope to make some positive suggestions.

Occasionally we hear reference to 'First Australian Nations'. I am ambivalent here. The notion that Australia as a continent was (prior to 1901) ever a single nation in the accepted sense of the term—'a unified group in dialogue with a common language'—has no credibility. The Tiwi and Tasmanians did not know of the other group's existence.

> Occasionally we hear reference to 'First Australian Nations'. I am ambivalent here. The notion that Australia as a continent was ... ever a single nation ... has no credibility.

We are aware of our nation's sad history: only about 20 of an original 200 plus languages are viable today and unless we take drastic national action in this respect, there will be no acceptable *lingua franca* in Australia, other than English, by about 2050.

But if First Australians wish to call their own clearly defined areas 'nations' and refer to themselves as 'First Nations people', that should become national practice. The

Warlpiri—one large identifiable group of First Australian people speaking one still viable Australian language—are recognised owners of an area of land much larger than Switzerland. They have every right to refer to themselves as 'a nation'. (Paradoxically, there are four languages spoken in Switzerland, but no nation matches the Swiss in matters of sovereignty and independence).

There is no conceivable chance of First Australians developing anything resembling title or sovereignty over the entire land mass of Australia. In the privacy of the ballot box 97 percent of the population will prevail. But specific groups have undeniable rights in their respective regions. The declaration of 'Heritage Nations' located within the constitutionally-authorised States and Territories of the Republic of Australia will be difficult to achieve; however, it is possible and must be addressed. The sad reality is that First Australians are currently disempowered; only a reasonable federal government can assist their empowerment. State governments, however supportive they may be, will be a hindrance in the biggest issue confronting the federal government.

The two words that I want to stay in all minds are: *land rights*. First uttered by First Australians in Victoria and New South Wales in the 1930s, these words reached usage at a national level in the Northern Territory in the 1960s, when the Yolngu clans of North East Arnhem Land and then the Gurindji at Wave Hill put their respective cases to the nation.

> The two words that I want to stay in all minds are: *land rights*.

The Yolngu clan leaders eventually went to the Courts. The Gurindji went to the people. Each scored a victory of sorts. The Yolngu lost the Court Case, but won the attention of the federal government under Whitlam; the Woodward Royal Commission into Aboriginal Land Rights was set up. The Gurindji were given a lease over a substantial area of Wave Hill Station, previously 'owned' by absentee landlord, Lord Vestey of England. After many years of to-ing and fro-ing, demos and physical punch-ups, the question of land rights was heard in the High Court and the irrefutable Mabo decision eventually negated the traditional *terra nullius* stance:

the High Court Judges decreed that Eddie 'Koiki' Mabo had established that he was the actual 'owner' of a tiny plot of land, on the basis of heredity, on Mer (Murray) Island in the Torres Strait. People have been singing: 'From little things big things grow' hopefully from that time, but the stark reality is that no single First Australian has actual sovereignty over a single square metre of land in Australia, on the basis of legally prescribed heredity or inheritance. There is much symbolism: there is no real justice.

It is time for some irrefutable action, authorised by government decree, to establish real, meaningful, permanent, land rights for First Australians, on the basis of accepted standards of 'inheritance'. Nobody queries the inherited succession rights of Prince Charles, Prince William and Co to be future Sovereigns of the United Kingdom. As members of the British Commonwealth we bow to them and deferentially address them as 'Your Majesties' and 'Your Royal Highnesses'. Even the somewhat ludicrous House of Lords commands our respect. The lines are known, sacrosanct. In Australia, nobody queries people who own land and assets the right to bequeath such 'property' to their descendants. Koiki Mabo's case was decided because he was able to establish valid inheritance, but no rules were written down, other than the vague recognition of a tiny block of land as 'traditional ownership'. When I organised an aircraft to fly Vincent Lingiari and other Gurindji elders around the Wave Hill region in 1971, in several unconnected flights on a charter aircraft, they read the country like a map and were unanimous—even though I asked the pilot of the aircraft to try to confuse them—in knowing where their traditional authority started and finished. 'No more … this one Mudbara country, this one Warlpiri country' Vincent and all others would say to the pilot. No doubt in their minds about their inheritance. All we had to do was ask.

Given that within the terms of the 1967 Referendum, the federal government now has paramount rights to introduce laws—benign laws—for the benefit and recognition of First Australians, the onus should be on the State and Territory governments to stand back and let long overdue justice be implemented by the Feds. I am perturbed by activists who call for the removal of the 'race clause' introduced in 1967. This is crazy: this is the means whereby the federal parliament can pass benign, positive legislation.

The High Court delivered the Mabo Judgment on the basis of a small, individual plea, thereby creating *ejusdem generis* national precedent. I suggest that in establishing 'land rights'—but this time incorporating sovereignty—on an acceptable, positive level, that a single *Heritage Nation* be used as the base for exploratory negotiations. I suggest the Tiwi Islands and the Tiwi Nation as our best opportunity to quickly—immediately in fact—create and set desirable national precedents.

My first semantic suggestion is to forget the word 'treaty'. Treaties are invariably drawn up by conquerors purporting to help, perhaps rehabilitate former adversaries. Treaties are inevitably one sided, often counter-productive. I suggest 'Mutual Recognition' as the stated quest and that an appropriate Australian word be established. Forget 'Makarrata'. Whitefellas and many First Australians can't pronounce the word properly and it is not an appropriate word in any case. A Makarrta (note spelling) is a trial by ordeal—often called 'payback'—involving blood letting. Makarr translates as 'thigh', makarrta as 'into the thigh'. In 1957 I saw an actual Makarrta in Arnhem Land; while I acknowledge that sometimes the ritual thigh-spearing restores peace, the ceremony I saw resulted in years of vindictive retribution.

In the case of the Tiwi—having been given permission from the Tiwi Land Council—I recommend that Australia has the opportunity to lead the world in positive recognition of the original inhabitants of land; this can be achieved by the "Mutual Recognition of Legal Constitutions".

A Constitution does not need to be a *written* document. There is a written Australian Constitution (1901), based largely on the written United States Constitution (enacted in 1789). But, while Australia and

USA derive their systems of government from the British, there is no written Constitution in the United Kingdom. Yes, there is a Constitution, but it is a 'body of law' based on evolving centuries of positive, benign government. No single document.

The Tiwi have lived on their islands for countless thousands of years; they have had a Constitution, a 'body of law'—known to them as *Tuwitiya*—which dates back to a time before the presence of human beings in the British Isles. Tuwitiya was certainly in practice long before the development of the language known as English.

Here are notes re Tuwitiya. I stress that it does not purport to be the Tiwi Constitution: there is *no* written Tiwi Constitution. This is simply a manifesto, approved in principle by the Tiwi Land Council. These notes were compiled for the Tiwi Land Council by Ted Egan (Murrumungatjimirri) advised by Sister Tess Ward, Magdalen Kelantumama, Fiona Kerinaua and Leonie Tipiloura.

TUWUTIYA

Kapi parlingarri purumuwu kapi awungarra nanki yiraya ratuwati. Ngawa yati nimarra ngimpirimi nginingawula ngapangiraga. Nginingawula murrakupuni kapi waya winga awunipapurti, api ngawa Tiwi nginingawula. Ngawa Tiwi wangatamiya ngarumuwu kapi nginaki murrakupuni. Ningani ngawa Tiwi ngawa wantirrana arikurtumurnuwi. Ngawa Tiwi warntirrana ngapwulipirri ngini parlingarri ngawa-ampi, amintiya ngawa-maninguwi putuwurupuwa. Nanki yiraya ratuwati purumamula Bathurst amintiya Melville Islands. Waya ningani yintanga aripurriti Tiwi Islands. Ngawa karluwu yoni yintanga ngaripurriti.

Nginingawula ngirramini ngini ngawa-ampi, ngawa-maninguwi, ngawa-rringanuwi putuwurupura api awarra ngawurrayapunya. Tuwutiya arnungka jurra. Awarra nanki ngini Purrukuparli yimi parlingarri api awarra ngawurranungurumagi. Waya ningani wurrukurrunyuwi amintiya alalinguwi ngini pimatapiliga nginingawula Tiwi ngirramini.

Nginingajingawula Tiwi ngarumulungurrumani, api yiminga ngapapurikaga ngini ngawa-maninguwi amintiya ngawa-naruwi yiminga. Ngawa-ampi, ngawa-rringanuwi ngini wutawa murrakupuni lapi apingimi, api ngawa wiyarri nginingawula murrakupuni, awunganuwanga ngini yoyi ngarimi.

Parlingarri karluwu pirimarrumuwani angi wuta ngirimika, pili awarra arikularni ngirramini arima. Parlingarri ngirramini putuwurupura ngini purrumarrumuwani pinginginta mamirnikuwi. Waya ningani ngapapunya angi pupuka jarrumwaka.

Nginingajinawula Tiwi ngarikiyamama awungarra. Karrikuwapi pimatimi ngini wutawa wurrumamiliya.

Tiwi ngirramini ngini ngawurrayapunya ngini parlingarri ngawa-ampi putuwurupura ngini Tuwitiya pirikirimani.

Ngini Tiwi wangatamiya ngirramini wurikirimi ngini kutakaminawurti, waya juwa ngini pupuni ngirramini, api wuta papurrluwi kuwa wurimi.

Ngarra awarra ngwurranungurumagi ngini kapi ngawa-ampi putuwurupura.

Tuwitiya: Tiwi Constitution
(English) translation of the above paper

The Tiwi people of northern Australia have lived on our two major islands for countless centuries—parlingarri. We are one people and we speak one language. Our land is clearly defined by the sea. We were isolated so precisely from the other people of the universe that we did not see the need to establish a collective name for ourselves. Today we are called Tiwi, but that word simply identifies we human beings—tiwi—as distinct from the flora, fauna and other phenomena that are also recognised as component sharers in our culture. Our two major islands are known as Bathurst and Melville Islands—latterly as 'The Tiwi Islands'—but we have never seen the need to give separate names to these two islands.

Our society has always abided by the Tiwi Constitution—Tuwitiya—that has been in place for centuries. Our Constitution is not contained in a written document, but it comprehensively covers the system of principles and laws whereby our land is governed. The terms are known to all of us, handed down by our ancestor Purrukuparli for the guidance of our elders, aluwurra and aluwurringa, *who* are required to keep Tiwi law strong and sacred.

In Tiwi society, every person is born with a personal name—yintanga—and a lifelong, prescribed, dual identity. A person's yiminga (identity) derives from the mother; to prevent inbreeding, a person may not marry a person of the same yiminga. A person's responsibility to land derives from the murrakupuni (clan) of the father.

In past times our society condoned polygynous unions and promised marriages, but since the early 1900s those practices were discontinued. Today, there is gender equality among our people in all matters.

In Tiwi society everyone is equal before the law and no person is above the law. A good life is prescribed for all.

There are laws concerning marriage and inheritance of land. There are acknowledged and prescribed stages of learning. Our laws are perpetuated via the songs and the ceremonies associated with the good management of the land. These ancient songs and ceremonies are known to appropriate people and they record our origins and history.

There are conventions to provide for care and custody of those in need.

There are prescribed rules and conventions to resolve disputes and to restore harmony thereafter.

There is strong scientific evidence that supports our claim to exclusive, long-term, unique, isolated governance of our islands.
(End of translation)

It is relatively easy for the federal government to recognise Tuwitiya. The Tiwi are reasonable people, they live on land that is clearly defined by the sea; they speak one traditional language; there is no counter-claim to their land. Their track record says that they are law-abiding people; they know their own laws; additionally, they respect the laws of the Australian Commonwealth (est. 1901) and those of the new Northern Territory government (est. 1981).

First Australians? Nations? There are other nations/tribes of First Australians still speaking traditional languages as 'first language', living in defined areas—mostly in the proposed new state of North Australia where there is no competitive claim over their land. Given a 'standard procedure' established first with the Tiwi, it would be relatively easy to define such *Heritage Nations*, identify the actual names of members and put in place the means of assisting that Nation to affluent autonomy.

I acknowledge that in other areas within Australia, particularly around larger cities, where traditional language is gone and cultural observances are diminished, it will be extremely complicated to provide justice. There is, however, little doubt that members of different traditional groups have always known who belongs to whom. Kinship is still the most common topic of discussion among most First Australians:

as Mandawuy Yunupingu once said to me: 'We speak of little else'.

If the Tindale Map of Traditional Languages is used as a guideline, it will be easy for First Australians themselves to identify as nations. The general practice throughout traditional Australia is that your 'identity' is established matrilineally, because that fact is indisputable: your mother is your mother. Your responsibility to land derives patrilineally. See the Tiwi example above.

It would be relatively easy for a new Republican government to recognise the various Australian Heritage Nations.

The highly accredited First Australian, Ms Pat Turner AM, quite rightly asserts the need for self-determination by her people, in order to actually 'close the gap'. Especially in the dispossessed regions, in defining and establishing nations, there will be the initial requirement for the federal government to provide sufficient funding to enable important, relevant issues to be accommodated.

> It would be relatively easy for a new Republican government to recognise the various Australian Heritage Nations.

Again, New Zealand can provide meaningful tactics for Australia to follow. There are obvious impediments to Maori claims to total ownership of the country. Maori people acknowledge their migration southward to Aotearoa from their Polynesian origins; the establishment of hundreds of autonomous *marae* recognises the affiliation of various groups in their occupancy of the new land. An obvious requirement in Australia will be to establish a similar 'sovereign home base' and the title to 'Heritage Land' of appropriate size. That will be complicated, but is achievable.

14   Full Nationhood

There is no doubt that in Australia, prior to 1788, over 200 traditional languages were spoken. There were some common dialects, nowadays referred to as the *lingua franca* of a specific region, like Gupapuyngu in north-east Arnhem Land, but by and large the various languages were separate entities. The Tasmanian and Tiwi (NT) languages—spoken by the two groups living at the southern and northern extremities of the continent—did not have a single common word. Indeed, those two groups knew nothing of one another's existence.

> **There is no doubt that in Australia, prior to 1788, over 200 traditional languages were spoken.**

No traditional group in Australia had a specific name for the entire continent as the world knows it today.

Hence it is nonsense to speak of 'an Australian nation' prior to 1901, because there is no traditional word that matches the adopted word 'Australia', which derives from Latin. The place name 'Australia'—to describe the mainland and the various adjacent islands including Tasmania was introduced by the explorer, Matthew Flinders.

There is heated debate in Australia about the most appropriate day to recognise as 'Australia Day'. Dates discussed seem to be restricted to 26 January (the present gazetted Australia

Day); 25 April (Anzac Day); and 1 January (Federation Day). There are many reasons why none of these three dates is suitable as a day revered by all Australians as our 'national day'.

26 January was only recently gazetted as Australia Day by the Howard Government. There is a concerted move to discredit this day, now contemptuously termed 'Invasion Day'. The movement is led by First Australians, many sincere, but not acknowledging—in most cases—that a major percentage of their individual DNA scores derives from the invaders whom they vilify, their own white ancestors. Their campaign is marred by the inevitable presence of Rent a Mob members, out for friction on any issue going. This minority movement has limited credibility; its supporters seem unable/unwilling to offer a suitable alternative date, acceptable to the majority of our citizens, to establish a day of national celebration. They simply seek 'division'. The date does not have much credibility in any case. In Jewish 'single name' terms, 26 January might well be called *Hangover* as Captain Phillip's flag raising on 26 January 1788 was followed by rum-fuelled debauchery among the soldiers and convicts.

The 25 April date is the anniversary of two important military exercises, firstly the aggressive invasion at Gallipoli by the Anzacs seeking to capture Turkey in 1915. The same date is also the anniversary of the courageous participation by Australians in the defence (1918) of Villers-Bretonneux (France)—a truly heroic victory that helped bring an end to World War One. 25 April, while important in military terms, should be a day of observance (on two counts) not celebration: joint observance with New Zealand in respect of Gallipoli and observance with Britain, France, New Zealand and Canada in respect of Villers-Bretonneux.

1 January is the date on which the Australian Federation was proclaimed, based on a national Constitution, in which it was decreed that, in reckoning the national population figures, 'Aboriginal natives of Australia shall not be counted': they were deemed to be a sub-species. Additionally, on that date,

the self-styled Fathers of Federation (all white, elderly males) bequeathed to us an inflexible Constitution, a hotch-potch of railway gauges, trading impedimenta and selfish clauses destined to preserve power for themselves within their various states and through their political parties. 1 January is an important date, but hardly a national day of celebration—other than as New Years Day.

On 8 September 1803 Matthew Flinders officially reported to Governor King that he and his crew had circumnavigated the island continent, *Terra Australis*. He used the name *Australia* for the first time. His maps are valid to this day. His Journals deserve study by every Australian.

The magnificent journals of Flinders indicate that he had recorded dialogue with First Australians in many of the coastal regions he visited. He was accompanied by Bungaree, a First Australian man from the Sydney region. Flinders deferred absolutely to Bungaree in traditional cultural matters; they accurately, impressively wrote down words of some of those distinctive coastal languages. Importantly, the journey was completed with minimal violence.

A vital fact connected to the date 8 September is that Bungaree is the first person born in Australia to have circumnavigated Australia. He is also the first First Australian to call this land Australia: Flinders and other crew members were born in England. The fact that Bungaree is also a First Australian by inheritance should cause him to be revered by all of us.

> **A vital fact connected to the date 8 September is that Bungaree is the first person born in Australia to have circumnavigated Australia.**

Matthew Flinders died in London in 1814. Bungaree died in Sydney in 1840 and is buried at Rose Bay. In 2019 Matthew Flinders' remains were discovered during diggings to extend Euston Station. It has been decided that he will be re-buried at Donington, Lincolnshire in the grounds of St Mary's Church, where he was baptised.

I suggest that statues of Flinders and Bungaree together be erected at Circular Quay, Sydney, to commemorate the start and finish of their circumnavigation. I recommend that the honorific *Conditor Australis*—or better, a First Australian term decided by the First Australian Academy—be bestowed on these two, called hereafter the Founders of Australia.

Prior to 1803 the land we now call Australia was still regarded primarily as a convict settlement and usually referred to by the English government as either Botany Bay or New South Wales. It was not until 1814 in London that the excellent charts compiled by Flinders prompted suggestions for the establishment of colonies for private British settlers in other parts of the great land mass.

I propose that 8 September is henceforth celebrated annually as Foundation Day—with yet another public holiday, enjoyed by all! Australians, let us rejoice, for we're a lucky country. Here is the last verse of my song Foundation Day:

> Circumnavigation, two busy years have passed
> Round the west coast, across the Bight,
> Back to Sydney at last:
> Returning to Port Jackson, tumultuous acclaim,
> We've charted an island continent
> Australia's its name
> Yes, we've charted an island continent
> Australia's its name!

15 THE LANGUAGE KNOWN AS AUSTRALIAN?

THE FIRST PERSON TO SPEAK AUTHORITATIVELY ABOUT THE number and diversity of the many traditional Australian languages was Norman Tindale; in 1940 he published a map of Australia, with attributed languages covering the entire continent. This has become a contentious issue, disputed by mining and pastoral companies and people opposed to First Australian recognition; Tindale is also discredited by some scientists. First Australians have varied opinions on Tindale and the general question of boundaries.

But there is no doubt that there are many people who continue to identify with old languages relating to specific areas throughout the nation; there are many thousands of First Australians who still speak around fifty of those as 'first' languages. A small number (probably fewer than twenty) of traditional languages are now written down, are being studied by both First Australian and other scholars, researched and thereby are retained for posterity.

There is also a lot of humbug, brought on by the preparedness of guilt-stricken governments—as well as quite worthy philanthropic bodies—to provide extensive funding to 'rehabilitate' languages that, sadly, might be lost forever. It might not be enough that grandma remembers the traditional word for 'kangaroo'. At the same time I acknowledge that for many years, in areas where traditional languages are still first languages for the locals, there have been many First Australian people seeking to teach their languages to their children in school situations.

Apart from justifiable claims by First Australians that 'these are the oldest languages in existence' this nation does not enjoy a reputation as speakers of languages other than English. Our next door neighbours are 250,000,000 Indonesians, but very few Australians know anything of Indonesian languages or culture. Very few Australians can even say 'G'day' in traditional Australian languages.

I ask non-Aboriginal children: 'Can you speak Australian? They usually respond: 'Howyergoinmate?' We all talk of 'Waltzing Matilda' but it has German origins. We all say 'fair dinkum' which derives from Cantonese. We have no songs in our traditional language that we all know and love to sing at 'international' gatherings, no books of consequence that we can read aloud with ease, teach to our children. We know all the standard English and American books of value. There are many Australian literary works of value, many fine songs and poems, but all are written in English.

At my instigation, in 1971 Galarrwuy Yunupingu AM gave a lengthy talk on land rights at the National Press Club, Canberra. He spoke in his first language (Gumatj) for around fifteen minutes, then said: 'Thank you for your patience. I gave you my message in my first language, Australian: I shall now translate into the introduced language, English'. He brought the house down!

In 1974 I organised a team of three First Australian groups, Tiwi, Djauan and Torres Strait Islanders, to attend the South Pacific Festival at Rotorua, New Zealand. We stayed at Maori *Maraes*. The Australians immediately perceived the impact of the eloquent speeches in the Maori language that always preceded every gathering. The three Australian leaders immediately fell into the pattern and performed similarly, impressively.

New Zealand has shown us how to do the bi-lingual stuff. Their Maori leaders have established an amalgamation of the introduced Polynesian languages—spoken by the various tribes who came to Aotearoa—as *THE* Maori Language. It is written, available to the world in Google Search.

All New Zealanders can 'small talk' in Maori—'*Kia Ora, Aroha,*' etc. Many—both Polynesian and Pakeha citizens—admirably talk and sing fluently in both Maori and English. They turned their somewhat dirgeish 'God Defend New Zealand' into a musical masterpiece when they wisely decided to sing the first verse of their National Anthem in Maori, the second time around in English. It now sounds magnificent. They now have two official languages: "Maori" and "English".

In 2006 I asked Alison Nararula Anderson, a First Australian, an elected Member of the Northern Territory Legislative Assembly to assist me in translating Australia's national anthem into a traditional language. Nararula is indeed a fine scholar: she should be awarded an Honorary Professorship. She is fluent and literate in at least five traditional languages, as well as English. She chose to translate into Luritja—an interesting choice: she went for Luritja in that 'it is not a threat to anybody'. The result is *Kutju Australia*. 'Kutju' is a brilliant word: it can be the numeral 'one'; it can establish 'pride of place in the pecking order': 'Kutju! Number One!' It can be 'Go' in terms of endeavour—'Kutju Tiges' sayeth the Richmond barracker. It certainly means 'advance', thus 'Kutju Australia'.

KUTJU AUSTRALIA
(*Literal translation*)

Anangula a tjutala
All people: rejoice
Unparri yingila
We are young, free

> Manta ngangka win'kingkula
> *[It is] Strong country, understood [by us]*
> Kapi puntu tjara
> *Water surrounds the land*
> Nanarri puntu ngurrangka
> *[We are] surrounded by good things*
> Puturrna kulinyi
> *[We know] the history of our country*
> Irriditja a wan'kara
> *From the olden times*
> Kutju Anangula
> *[So] go forward, people*
> Kutjuringla a warrala
> *Go forward together*
> Kutju Australia
> *Advance, Australia.*

We organised a video, whereby children from Ntaria (Hermannsburg NT) taught the children of Killara school (Sydney) to sing the song in Luritja. We recorded the process and published a book, CD, DVD and Teaching Notes. Assisted by the affluent Killara School Council, we brought the Killara children to the Northern Territory to meet the children of Ntaria: a joyful experience.

In the book we stressed that we were not seeking to 'impose' Luritja on any other traditional language group; we simply wanted to demonstrate that such a presentation was possible throughout Australia if that was the desire of the various language owners. Peter Garrett, then federal Minister for Education, enthused, said he wanted a copy of *The Kutju Kit* – book, CD, DVD, Teaching Notes – 'in every school in Australia'. He provided the funding. We delivered the goods.

The outcome was interesting. Only a few schools acknowledged receipt; a very small number enthused. Quite a few schools returned the attractive package unopened, probably suspicious that an invoice might follow. A friend in NSW, a talented music teacher in a school with many First Australian pupils, thought it would be a good song for her school choir, but was quickly rebuffed by the local Council of Indigenous Elders (speaking in English!), who told her not to teach 'that foreign lingo in our country'. We received a hostile reception in Victoria from groups who informed us (in English) that they were busy revitalising their own languages. Indeed at the Port Fairy Folk Festival that year, a children's choir sang the anthem in Gunditjmara, their local language.

Copyright in respect of the Australian National Anthem is held by the Department of the Prime Minister and Cabinet in Canberra. I wrote to the Secretary of the Department in 2008 suggesting the option of allowing—even encouraging—the National Anthem to be presented in approved First Australian languages, as well as English, as in New Zealand. I still await a reply to my letter. A simple acknowledgement would have been appreciated. Whatever happened to public service protocol?

The official Australian National Anthem has two verses in English; the second verse incorporates the nonsensical lines:

- For those who've come across the seas
- We've boundless plains to share …

Oh, yeah??? Tell that to the famous Biloela-based Sri Lankan refugee family, who made the mistake of arriving by sea.

A bi-lingual version of the national anthem remains a very worthy idea. I am convinced that we could develop a single traditional language, one widely spoken, researched, comprehensive yet sufficiently uncomplicated—and refer to it henceforth as *THE* Australian language, known thereafter as 'Australian'. That would give it official status: *Australian*, taught as a compulsory subject in all schools, encouraged in all areas of life. There are perhaps 10 traditional Australian languages that are written down, recorded to the required levels of sophistication. So which of these languages could be chosen? Without a doubt First Australians themselves will demand the final say on this issue. I applaud that.

> … we should develop a single traditional language, one widely spoken, researched, comprehensive yet sufficiently uncomplicated — and refer to it henceforth as *THE* Australian language, known thereafter as 'Australian'.

This might be one for The First Australian Academy? For what it is worth, as an example, I will make a case for Pitjantjatjara, usually shortened to Pitjantjara, as the best prospect. Again, I do not propose 'neglecting' or 'putting down' other traditional languages: on the contrary, the procedures involved in recognising one language as the official language to be called 'Australian' could provide the means whereby other languages could be enhanced and still proudly used by the members of the various Nations. Children especially take delight in the study of different languages. My twin great grand-daughters, at age four, switch easily from English to Polish to German. They moved recently from Munich to London. When Covid permits I shall teach them songs in Australian.

Pitjantjatjara is the principal language of the area known as 'The Western Desert' that covers an extensive area in WA, South Australia and NT. It began to be written down in the 1940s by Presbyterian missionaries based at Ernabella, South Australia.

In 1961 eminent American linguist Dr Ken Hale established that Pitjantjara is 'recognised' by most First Australians in the vast area ranging from Alice Springs (NT) to Broken Hill (NSW) to Adelaide (SA) to Kalgoorlie (WA) to Broome (WA), now often called 'outback Australia'. It is an easy language to speak: the only tricky sound is the occasional *ng* start to words, but once accomplished, that sound is a breeze.

Most importantly, orthographers have not ruined the prospect for the Pitjantjara language to be widely understood, written accurately, spoken easily. The Pitjantjara language can be written using the same Latin alphabet as English, typed on standard word processors.

A story worth telling. In 1966 in north-east Arnhem land there was a battle between the Yolngu (First Australians) and the mining company Nabalco, over the name for the proposed new township. The Yolngu said that the name bestowed by the spirit ancestor Wuyal should be used. The miners said the town should be called 'Gove', to honour an RAAF pilot of that name, killed in an air crash in the region in WWII. It was agreed that, if the Yolngu prevailed, the town would have a Yolngu matha (traditional language) name. The orthographers then got into the act. I said the name of the town should have the spelling Noolanboy, an accurate pronunciation, easy to accommodate. The orthographers spoke of 'an aspirated 'h' and a 'rounded suffix' and demanded Nhulunbuy as the spelling. It is on the map as Nhulunbuy, but, as most people have problems saying the word, the town is usually called Gove.

I can't speak Pitjantjara, but I am a good parrot and have used the language in a couple of songs I have recorded. I can verify that children of all backgrounds love to learn the words of those songs and are usually delighted at how easy it is. A wise Irish-born Australian friend recently passed the pertinent remark: 'Pitjantjara is the Mandarin of Australia'. I agree. Keep alive all surviving languages, but concentrate first on a national *lingua franca* known and loved by all Australians.

For starters, here is the present National Anthem in Pitjantjara:

> SONG
> (*Literal translation*)
>
> Anangu uwankarangku
> *Everyone join in*
> Pukultu inkama
> *Sing for joy*
> Manta wirula kanyini
> *We have a beautiful land*
> Urungka ngururpa
> *Surrounded by ocean*
> Mai winkitjara nguranka
> *There is abundant food*
> Wirunya mulapa
> *It is truly bountiful*
> Kuranyukutu wirura
> *Take good care together*
> Kanyinma tjungungku

> *Into the future*
> Pukularira inkama
> *Rejoice and sing*
> Australianya kutju
> *Australia, go forward*

The title of this book is *Kulilkatima*, a Pitjantjatjara word that translates into English as 'seeking understanding'. It is also the opening line of my song: '*This Land Australia*'. Kulilkatima ngura nyangatja: Try to understand this land Australia. All together now!

16 Wealth for First Australian Nations

In Chapter 13 I recommended the recognition of the Tiwi people as the first declared and defined First Australian Heritage Nation.

Although I travelled extensively throughout Australia and the Torres Strait Islands during my many years of service in Aboriginal Affairs, I shall concentrate on Northern Territory groups to indicate how a national campaign may be implemented. I have, by comparison, little specific knowledge of other areas.

I propose mutual recognition by the Tiwi people, the Commonwealth of Australia and the Northern Territory Government of each other's ongoing Constitutions. Next, I suggest that the Commonwealth and the Warlpiri people be invited to follow suit. The Warlpiri are a sizeable (approximately 2500 of the full descent) mainland group already recognised as the 'traditional owners' of a surveyed, described body of land. In those two processes—Tiwi, then Warlpiri recognition—many precedents will be established, an example for other groups to follow.

> I propose mutual recognition by the Tiwi people, the Commonwealth of Australia and the Northern Territory Government of each other's ongoing Constitutions.

It seems to me crucial that such relatively straight-forward recognition of Heritage Nations should quickly create recognisable, positive economic outcomes as an immediate consequence of the new partnership. I am going to sound dictatorial, but for starters, I think it essential that the land under the direct control of the new First Australian Nations is called Heritage Land. There should also be mutual agreement that *Heritage Land* may *never be sold*: leased, yes, and to the owner's advantage, but never to be sold or in any way totally alienated.

So, what is immediately available, to enable the Tiwi, the Commonwealth and the Northern Territory government to combine and achieve impressive commercial and social outcomes: jobs and money?

It is not for me to plan in detail, but the Tiwi already have many commendable economic activities in hand: forestry, wood chip exports, a functional port on Melville Island. They welcome tourists, they have land and sea rights that enable them to control fishing activity around their islands on a very reasonable level. They negotiate with the Commonwealth Defence Department to secure contracts of different kinds, as Australia's defence is now more logically based in north Australia. Given sovereign rights over their land, the Tiwi could encourage companies and individuals to lease land and come to their country on local terms, to ultimate local advantage: shopping centres, motels, housing societies, horticulture, marine farms, tourism, the arts, whatever. The Tiwi have an impressive relationship with the Australian Football League (AFL) which can be nurtured at popular and financially benign levels.

> ... there could be an engineering project of huge international relevance: harness the immense tidal movements that move in and out of Apsley Strait four times a day, every day.

Within the present concentration on climate change, there could be an engineering project of huge international relevance: harness the immense tidal movements that move in and out of Apsley Strait four times a day, every day. Apsley Strait is the narrow waterway that separates the two principal islands—Bathurst Island and Melville Island. Sufficient power could be generated to service the entire Tiwi needs and probably the nearby city of Darwin as well.

Harnessing solar and wind power is also a must on the Tiwi Islands.

The Warlpiri mainlanders are the recognised traditional owners of land that stretches from north west of Alice Springs, through the Tanami Desert to Lajamanu (Hooker Creek). This land is usually described as 'arid' but it is nonetheless extremely *valuable* in the true sense of that term. The Warlpiri know and understand their land, its features, its creatures. They have survived there for countless centuries: the land is not empty. If encouraged to stay on their own country and use it for their own benefit, the Warlpiri are capable of remaining intact as a 'tribal' traditional group; that in itself is a huge plus in world terms. They own and still use as their first language one of the oldest languages in the world. They still initiate all boys and girls into an acceptable, respected traditional system, known and approved by all members. They too can lay claim to a Constitution older than the English language. Any of the beneficial things that have been caused to happen in Israel are available to the Warlpiri, on their terms—harnessing solar and wind power, mining, pastoral pursuits, horticulture, tourism, student research—as well as the opportunity to keep alive all their traditional practices. In cultural areas they have created a wonderful, admirable festival at Lajamanu, titled 'Milperri', whereby they merge with Tracks Dance Company of Darwin to present traditional Yapa (Aboriginal) dancing and singing alongside today's young Hip-Hoppers and Rappers at an authentic, Warlpiri-oriented level. The enthusiasm is impressive.

If we can legislate for sovereignty in the approved Heritage Nations, a clever move would be to simultaneously declare the regions also as National Parks, with the arbitrary federal government requirement for the appointment and full time employment of First Australian rangers and trackers.

I have been urging Northern Territory Police for years to create a team of 'Trackers' and have them on hand, available

> **Harnessing solar and wind power is also a must on the Tiwi Islands.**

'on call' for any situation where tracking expertise is needed. Tracking was once an impressive factor of outback policing, but the employment of expert trackers has long been forsaken. I envisage that the people who would best qualify for these important positions would be elderly First Australian women, average age 50 plus. Forget the men. Bring in the experts. Cases like Chamberlain and Falconio would have been 'read' in a given hour: instead, dozens of well-intentioned police and volunteers tramped somewhat mindlessly over the terrain, obliterating vital clues.

Let me share a story. In 1965 I was teaching at Newcastle Waters. I walked to the school early one morning as the pupils assembled. Our old First Australian helper, Duncan, rushed to me: 'Keep the kids away!' he ordered. 'Why, what's wrong?' I asked. He pointed to the ground, to a long, impressive track in the dirt. 'Big snake', he said. Duncan and a couple of his male mates began, flamboyantly, to follow the track around the front of the school building. The children and I were duly impressed. Around the corner came Elsie, Duncan's wife. She took in the scene and began to laugh.

'Don't you laugh', I admonished her: 'They're tracking a big snake'.

'That true. Snake alright', she replied and pointed; 'But him bin go other way'. She walked to the back of the school, tracked the snake, cooked it for her lunch.

There are three areas where First Australians are more than equals: music, sport and knowledge of the environment. Let's acknowledge that, throughout the nation. They are the perfect public servants: they want to stay on country.

There has been in overall First Australian society a lamentable departure by people from their traditional homelands, over many years, for many understandable reasons. I am wary of generalisations, but I am happy to go on record and say: to separate First Australians from their country does them no favour.

In the 1960s, thousands of other Australians supported First Australians in

> **There are three areas where First Australians are more than equals: music, sport and knowledge of the environment. Let's acknowledge that ...**

their first national endeavours to get justice in their own country: 'What do we want? Land rights! When do we want it? Now!!!' became the catchcry. I was vitally involved in those days and those activities: although I was a public servant, I was never dissuaded from demonstrating with my many First Australian friends and contacts. There is no doubt in my mind that the most effective First Australian activist in those memorable days was Charles 'Chicka' Dixon aka 'The Fox'. What a man! He was Mandela-like: surprisingly cordial, always innovative, humorous, well-informed, ten steps ahead of everybody else from whatever quarter.

> 'What do we want? Land rights! When do we want it? Now!!!' became the catchcry.

Chicka Dixon's principal aim was to get recognition that (1) his people were here first; (2) his people, the First Australians, are here to stay, prepared to share their country with the various newcomers; (3) his people should be enabled to identify, then achieve proof of ownership of their traditional lands, or—if that is not totally possible—some recognition of a prior presence in their region, like the Maori people of New Zealand; (4) wherever possible, they should be encouraged to return to live in their own regions; and, (5) they should work co-operatively with the Australian government to rehabilitate their culture on their land, on their terms.

When I was a Commonwealth public servant, that was also the aim of the federal government. Sadly, all positive policy in respect of First Australians has now been abandoned: First Australians nowadays have to put up with *ad hoc*, fancy ideas proposed by supposedly smart whitefellas from think tanks.

Some of these projects get funded, most fail and the blackfellas get the blame: '... and we do so much for them' is the lament in government circles. First Australians in the Northern Territory 'own' one-third of the land mass, but instead of developing their own regions, many hundreds have drifted into the predictable role of fringe dwellers, living

Overleaf: A Working Future overview brochure, a Territory Government initiative 2012.

working future
A Territory Government initiative

A Working Future

A Working Future outlines a strong vision for remote areas. It's about government and local people working together to make our towns and communities better places to live.

A Working Future is the whole story of how government will work in remote areas of the Territory. It has six parts that join together.

A Working Future is the Territory Government's plan for improving the lives of remote Territorians. It is part of our Territory 2030 vision and will bring all Territorians together to create a dynamic, growing future for our community.

Part 1 Territory Growth Towns

Our biggest remote communities will become proper towns, with services, buildings and facilities like any other country town in Australia. These towns will become the economic and service delivery centres for their regions.

The 20 Territory Growth Towns will be:

Maningrida, Wadeye, Borroloola, Nguiu, Galiwin'ku, Milingimbi, Ngukurr, Angurugu/Umbakumba, Gunbalanya, Yirrkala, Numbulwar, Yuendumu, Hermannsburg, Ramingining, Gapuwiyak, Daguragu/Kalkarindji, Lajamanu, Papunya, Elliott and Ali Curung.

Part 2 Outstations and Homelands

The government will keep helping outstations and homelands with funding for services. The government will make sure that this money gets to residents for things they really need.

Outstations are mostly on private Aboriginal land, so the government will concentrate on helping residents and traditional owners to look after their own houses, bores and generators into the future. The government will not be building any new outstations.

For more information
www.**workingfuture**.nt.gov.au

working future
A Territory Government initiative

Part 3 — Remote Service Delivery

The Australian Government and the Territory Government will work together to provide services that local people need. We will have staff from both governments working together and have a 'one-stop shop' in our remote towns. Both governments will be looking at how they can work better to provide long-term funding so that communities can plan for the future with certainty.

Part 4 — Employment and Economic Development

Just like anywhere else in the world, our towns and communities need private investment to work properly. This includes local people owning their own businesses and homes to build up their wealth. And if we want private investment, we need to make sure that people and companies can get a long-term, secure lease for their shop, office, workshop or house. With this lease they can borrow money, build their businesses and sell their assets to make a profit.

The government will help local people plan for the future of their local economy and put in place strategies to attract and support new businesses. A long-term Indigenous Economic Development Strategy will help provide the right pathway.

Part 5 — Remote Transport Strategy

People in smaller communities need regular and affordable transport to get to jobs, schools, clinics, shops and other services in larger towns. The government will be working with local people on a Remote Integrated Transport Strategy to help make sure that people can get into the larger towns and get back home again safely.

Part 6 — Closing the Gap Targets and Evaluation

Governments need to prove they are achieving real results. All governments in Australia have agreed to a set of targets to 'close the gap' of Indigenous disadvantage, especially in remote areas. The Territory Government will report against the closing the gap targets every year. It will also have special evaluation of remote service delivery – to make sure it is really helping remote towns and communities achieve *A Working Future*.

> More information: If you want to know more about *A Working Future*, you can call us on 08 8999 5270 or contact your local Government Business Manager.

www.**workingfuture**.nt.gov.au

on the outskirts of cities and towns. They are bound in the clutches of Centrelink and other purportedly helpful agencies. That has happened elsewhere in Australia for 200 years: it must be stopped.

There was in the 1950s, 1960s and 1970s a concerted plan in the Northern Territory that a 'standard country town' would be established in every tribal area. They were ultimately called the 'Bob Beadman' towns, after the enterprising public servant given credit for pioneering the plan. In real terms, credit should first be given to a much-maligned man named Harry Giese. Giese was the Northern Territory's Director of Welfare from 1954 to 1972, when he was dismissed from his post by a gleeful Whitlam Labor government. Since that time Giese has been portrayed as the villain who sought to destroy traditional Aboriginal culture. That is quite unfair: he was certainly an autocrat, but one of his best achievements was to establish Eisteddfodau, which allowed many magnificent First Australian artists to get cultural recognition: performers like David Gulpilil, David Blanasi, Tjoli Laiwanga and the many dance groups.

The towns proposed by Giese, later by Bob Beadman, were to be 'models', each one having the same basic assets as a successful country town anywhere in Australia: a hospital, school, childcare centre, local housing society working towards good quality accommodation for all residents, sports facilities, motel, supermarket, paved roads, library, concert hall, police station, centre for rehabilitation, quality reticulated water, solar powered electricity. The principal aim was that local First Australian labour would be the workforce.

The map opposite shows locations of the proposed towns.

I will outline in Chapter 17 the reasons why First Australians generally are so unhealthy: I blame that principally on inadequate diet. In the Giese/Beadman towns there was to be a concentration on two things; trade training in all fields and domestic training, based on old-fashioned gender rules. Given appropriate sovereignty, there is nothing to prevent First Australian landowners from having the best available food

Wealth for First Australian Nations 93

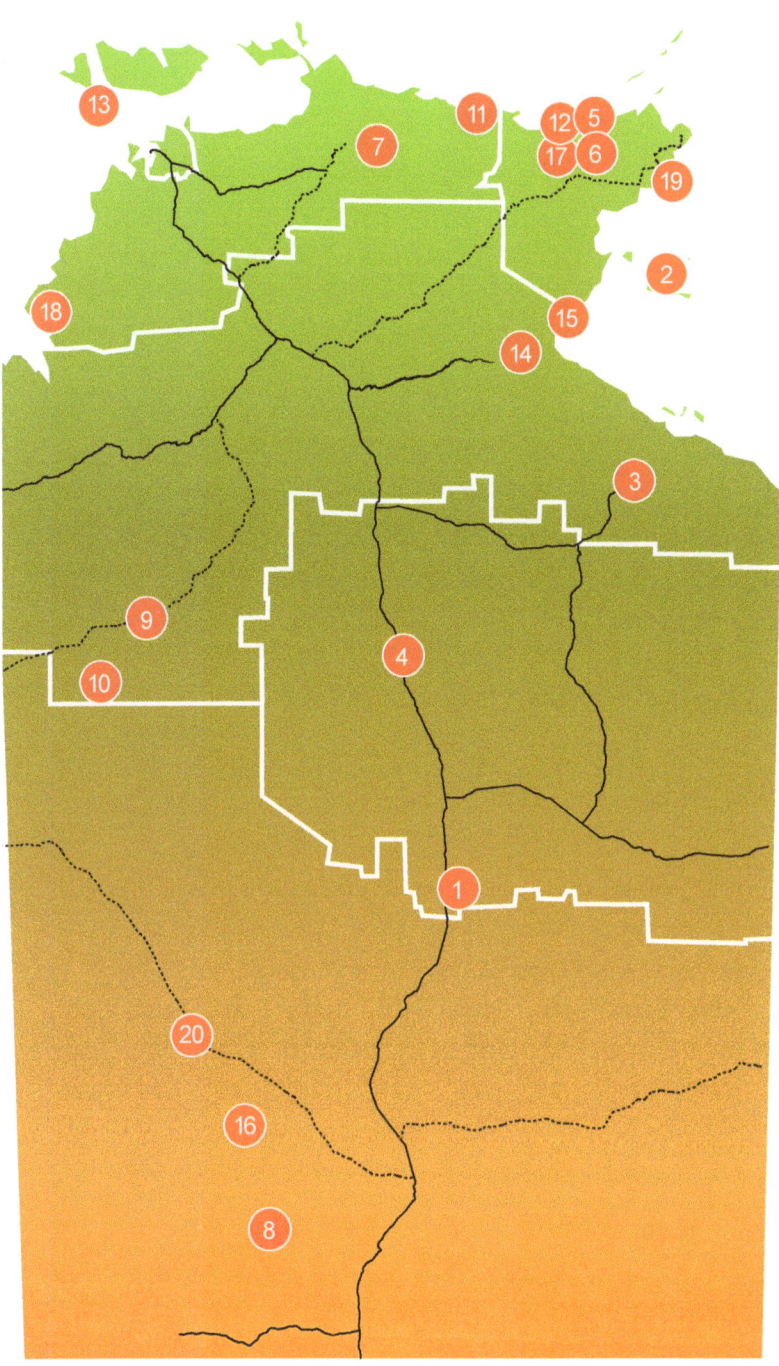

TERRITORY GROWTH TOWNS

1. Ali Curung
2. Angurugu and Umbakumba
3. Borroloola
4. Elliott
5. Galiwin'ku
6. Gupuwiyak
7. Gunbalanya
8. Ntaria (Hermannsburg)
9. Kalkarindji and Daguragu
10. Lajamanu
11. Maningrida
12. Milingimbi
13. Wurrumiyanga (formerly Nguiu)
14. Ngukurr
15. Numbulwar
16. Papunya
17. Ramingining
18. Wadeye
19. Yirrkala
20. Yuendumu

franchises in their towns, as well as being reared in traditions of best use of sensible houses that they own, rather than rent. Indeed, it is both feasible and desirable that real owners of First Australian land can lease areas for expert farming, agricultural, horticultural. and pastoral practice, together with training of local First Australians.

Sadly, by 2020, after seventy years of promises, not a single town of consequence was ever completed, despite the bestowal (purported) of billions of taxpayer dollars and countless, meaningless 'training courses' run by power-pointing public servants Many houses and other substantial buildings have been constructed, invariably by contractors who declined to employ local workers: as a consequence there is no local pride in 'our town'. Houses are abandoned if somebody dies therein, dogs assume residence, former residents move away, children wreck the buildings. Given no financial or physical input by or from locals, the standard mendicant attitude prevails: 'Government will provide, because we are Aboriginals. They'll build us more houses'. Over and over again.

> ... by 2020, after seventy years of promises, not a single town of consequence was ever completed, despite the bestowal (purported) of billions of taxpayer dollars and countless, meaningless 'training courses' ...

Nurses and school teachers are hard to find and keep on the job, as conditions are not good. There is often physical danger for staff; local health and education standards suffer accordingly. Today, First Australians from those bush areas—denied the standard entitlements of life in their homelands—are living around Darwin, Alice Springs, Katherine, Tennant Creek and Nhulunbuy. Fringe dwelling is a self-fulfilling prophecy, bringing demoralisation and degradation. That has been the sad outcome throughout Australia for the previous 200 years Many such refugees have no alternative lifestyle available, given the absence of bush hospitals, ante—and post-natal birth centres, dialysis clinics. The large town hospitals do a remarkable job, but are totally overburdened.

Around these bigger towns the visiting First Australians—traditionally treated as 'foreigners' and subject to known rules and conventions—are exposed to overcrowding in sordid 'town camps'; they are subject to violence and intimidation, drug and alcohol addiction, hunger and exposure. With their only financial access restricted to minimal social service payments, adults and children run the risk of becoming involved in organised minor (sometimes very major) crime. Law abiding major town residents face the constant threat of house burglary, car theft, physical assault. Children do not attend school: why would they? Teenage gangs easily outrun police, who are clad in cumbersome uniforms, but powerless in real terms. The gaols, detention centres and prisons are full. The statistics are run before our eyes daily.

All these First Australians should be affluent, healthy, energetic, happy, able to get on with the real and important things of life in their ancient homelands. Given heritage sovereignty First Australians would be able to develop business opportunities, in their own right—in town development, housing societies, mining, horticultural, pastoral, cultural and tourism pursuits—all on their own terms. In addition, they should also be responsible for the apprehension/punishment/rehabilitation of criminals and offenders from their own Nation's membership. Therein lie the answers to all the current over-representation of First Australians in gaols and detention centres.

For almost thirty years (1974–2003) I presented the Ted Egan Outback Show at Alice Springs. The single most expressed wish of the hundreds of thousands of tourists that I entertained was: 'How do we meet First Australians on respectful terms?'

I feel confident that an Academy of First Australians would encourage the establishment of accessible Centres of Knowledge similar to the Cultural Centre at Uluru and the Garma Festival of Arnhem Land, where visitors can fulfil that wish, talking to knowledgeable Elders, visiting Art Galleries and museums, learning old languages at varying levels. Let valid traditional knowledge be recognised as the hallmark of the real Australia. This should be the basis of our national pride.

First Australian children and parents would see the reason for education. They deserve better than they are offered at the moment, as the gap widens. Where are you, Prime Minister?

17 Funding the Arts

There is a regrettable tendency in Australia, particularly with Conservative governments, to reduce funding, indeed privatise the ABC, their 'leftist' *bête noire*.

Let us hope that sanity prevails. It is acknowledged that the ABC 'ain't what it used to be' in many respects; but in its halcyon days it provided an excellent service for Australia generally and 80 million 'Pacific' listeners to Radio Australia. By all means review the ABC Estimates and look for unnecessary extravagances. Let's scale down on some of the so-called—but too often unfunny—comedy shows; but we should restore the mature international programs. Let's find today's Tim Bowden and commission radio documentaries like *Taim Bilong Masta* and *Prisoners Under Nippon*. Let's recruit and train, in the old-fashioned way, the latterday Ray Martin, Caroline Jones, Bill Peach, Peter Luck, Jana Wendt and other stars of the ABC in its halcyon 1970s.

With producers Ken Watts, Gerald Stone, Margaret Throsby, Tim Bowden, Caroline Jones, Stuart Littlemore, the ABC established shows like *This Day Tonight* (*TDT*) based on BBC counterparts, but delivered without plums in the mouth and with impeccable savvy. We need sufficient funding and staff to ensure that TV programs like *Four Corners* continue to expose corruption, collaboration and connivance. We need commentators of the calibre of Derek Guille and Geraldine Doogue to keep us informed, with pinpoint accuracy, in times of bushfires, floods or disasters.

I was fortunate to work direct to Dr H C 'Nugget' Coombs in his 'retirement' years. 'Nugget' had faithfully served successive Prime Ministers from the 1930s to the mid 1960s, as Governor of the Commonwealth and Reserve Banks, later as Director of Post War Reconstruction. Following the 1967 Referendum he agreed to be Chair of Prime Minister Holt's Council for Aboriginal Affairs. Simultaneously he became Chancellor of Australian National University and Chair of the Australia Council for the Arts, with the awesome Dr Jean Battersby as his CEO.

In his long and distinguished career Coombs had the knack of imposing his Keynesian economic beliefs on the 'finer things of life', often, surprisingly, to the pleasing outcome where seeming indulgence prompted economic, as well as artistic and social success. He loved to be surrounded by 'the beautiful people'.

What a combination Coombs and Battersby were! Australia has never seen initiative in the arts world to match those sparkling days. The Elizabethan Theatre Trust was founded and funded. The Aboriginal Arts Board was established. The Whitlam and Fraser governments generously funded most branches of the Arts. Hawke and Keating, following on, were also enthusiastic supporters: various ministers exhibited common sense and good taste

> **The Arts have become something of a governmental target. Funding has been savagely reduced.**

Since those days, however, we have failed to carry on. The Arts have become something of a governmental target. Funding has been savagely reduced. There are constant attacks on the Australian Broadcasting Commission by conservative governments: funds are diminished time and time again and the demand is for 'privatisation' which can be interpreted as 'gifted to the conservative owners of commercial TV, radio and press'. We seem to be living in hope that private philanthropy—American or European style—will provide funding for artistic endeavour. It does happen here, but not necessarily at a benign level. We occasionally see financial sponsorship of the arts—and sports—by mining companies, alcohol (previously tobacco) companies, and betting agencies—for quite devious, obvious reasons.

I advocate healthy tax concessions for worthy philanthropy. At the same time, I recommend that governments return to a more positive, more realistic attitude, particularly around music, at all levels.

Why is music so important? First and foremost, music is the fundamental factor in the lives of almost all human beings. The first meaningful thing that happens after the birth of a baby is the intense attention given to the participants, the mothers and the babies themselves, as the 'rhythms' of life are established. The movements of arms and legs, fingers and toes are scrutinised; it is an age-old introduction to life. From that moment the baby starts on a journey of expression of its feelings, that will be recognised as 'dancing' and 'singing' and become a vital measure of transformation to childhood, teenage, maturity, life and eventually death. Music will be a vital factor at all times, even for those who profess otherwise. Early in the child's life, it is highly likely that somebody will sing a lullaby, the standard way to invoke peaceful sleep. May we ever continue our singing. I love to sing and am likely to do so regardless!

In most societies, the entire childhood will develop around things musical. Nursery rhymes, school songs, catchy ditties, songs as components of games, formal music lessons, introduction to musical instruments. No matter how basic, all of these things are present in even the most impoverished schools.

Music involves the establishment of school orchestras, bands, dance classes for groups, prompts individual opportunities for talented performers, all of which will have a vital impact in adult life. Some of us will proceed to full time careers, most will develop affection for some form of musical appreciation, which will be crucial in 'my enjoyment of life'. My relaxation. My sanity.

The various individual roles created around music are as old as civilisation itself. Invariably we recognise 'troubadors' whose role is to ensure that the lifestyle of the particular group is presented via the established songs, or the creation of appropriate new songs. The Jewish cantors, the Celtic bards, the various Minstrels—Bob Dylan, John Charles Thomas, Joan Baez, Peter Dawson, Dolly Parton, Richard Tauber, Eric Bogle, Gurrumul Yunupingu, Joni Mitchell, K D Lang—and ???—please insert your choices. They excite us. They provoke us. They inform us. They stimulate our thoughts on crucial issues. They record the intimate detail of our history, they challenge us to confront the future.

Some countries are recognised as world advocates for various forms of music. Most nations—Australia a notable exception—are strong at singing at sporting contests. Bulgaria, England, Estonia, New Zealand and Wales are particularly famous for ethereal choir singing. Additionally, the leading nations of the world always produce so many individual musicians and singers. Italy and Spain have made a huge mark in the world, via their love and presentation of unforgettable operas. The USA and The Caribbean have given us jazz, big bands and reggae, all strongly derivative from Africa. Several South African friends have told me that the principal weapon opposing the evil policy of *apartheid* was the singing of African women. The UK saw The Beatles change the world and the various African and West Indian migrants now living in the UK have provided a new dimension to church choirs. The star performers, conductors and orchestras are too numerous to mention, but let us keep loving them, evaluating them, remembering them. One of the great advantages of the present times is the opportunity, in so many different ways, to retain recorded gems of our musical history, wherever, forever.

National anthems are a good indicator of the fervour of some nations. French people easily, tunefully and on all worthy occasions, are prepared to sing *La Marseillaise.* It is held in Rugby circles that *Hen Wlad Fy Nhadau* sung incomparably by 50,000 Welsh voices is worth five points at Cardiff Arms Park.

Shanty singing in its various forms, preserves the history of 'work songs'.

On a negative note, arch criminals like Goebbels, recognising the love of the German people for their musical heritage, created a sinister weapon for the Third Reich, as lethal as the Nazi movement itself. How dare he! What an insult to the composers.

Summing up, music is good for the soul. We all need it in our lives. It provides a tonic for our 'inner hearts' as our Scottish friends remind us. Och aye!

First Australian society has always catered for the people who know the old songs and keep singing them. They are not required to do anything else in life; they expect—and receive—the support and acknowledgement of the extended families to which they belong. Take a look at the video clip of Gurrumul Yunupingu, circulated after his untimely death: born blind, always in need of physical assistance, he was crucial to the ceremonial life of his people. There were two words always on his mind—'bunggul' (ceremony) and 'manikay' (song). Nothing else mattered. He knew he was needed. We are the beneficiaries.

In Tiwi society, such is the esteem accorded aluwirra and alawurringa (elders) that they are expected to compose what are called 'Kulama' (Yam) songs—around a ceremony of the same name—during which young people are advanced to a greater level of traditional knowledge. These are long, complicated chronologies, presenting current thoughts on recent events. It's called recording history.

The various forms of music have always presented challenges to the innovators. What joy has been brought into our lives by the composers, the musicians, the Conservatoria, the various schools of dance, festivals like the Edinburgh Tattoo, the brass bands on parade, the musical comedy societies, the singers of renown, the songwriters, the distributors, the entrepreneurs.

In particular, I recommend especial recognition of the

> **The various forms of music have always presented challenges to the innovators. What joy has been brought into our lives by the composers, the musicians, the Conservatoria, the various schools of dance, festivals ...**

magnificent dance company, Bangarra, initiated by the Page family of Queensland. Bangarra has wisely based its interpretation of First Australian culture on respectful study of age-old, traditional ceremonial dance. Thereby they present to the Western world a valid amalgamation of the old and the new, but at all times a unique 'only in Australia' understanding of 'the Dreamtime'. Old Europe-oriented ballet and opera companies deserve and seek the certainty of guaranteed funding at an appropriate level. They have had mixed success, given the uncertain attitudes to cultural activity of various governments. Bangarra has been less fortunate with funding, yet they have produced shows like *Benelong* and *Skin* that received tumultuous world acclaim.

I like to think that a body like The President's Academy would set the permanent, appropriate funding standards necessary to enable Australia to share the stage with the best in the world, also to encourage philanthropic guidance, accompanied by taxation benefit.

It is crucial that support be forthcoming, to enable all musical talent to be fostered to the ultimate level. We are all involved, but government members have a responsibility to promote musical enjoyment; they are elected to serve the people. The people need music in all its various forms.

Again, there is the paradox that investment in music can be termed a sensible, pragmatic approach, for huge financial outcomes often eventuate. Look at the amount of money raised by Bob Geldof and associates, via music, to provide commendable support for underprivileged countries. I have personally been involved in many concerts and fundraising campaigns for worthy causes; I remain available. Music engenders compassion; compassion is needed in the big scheme of things.

Look at the enhancement of the Tamworth region as an outcome of the courage of Max Ellis, John Minson, Nick Erby, Lorraine Pfitzner, June Smyth, the Tamworth City Council—and so many others—as they took the bold decision to establish Tamworth as 'The Country Music Capital of Australia'. So many other things have developed in the region as a consequence. What an earner it has been! What a challenge to other centres!

Around the many musical activities that deserve financial backing, jobs are created, careers develop, audiences attend, centres are built, tickets are sold, businesses are opened, regions thrive, journeys are travelled, equipment is purchased. Money makes the world go around, the world go around, the world go around ... all together now! Kutju!

All other artists of whatever form of performance, achievement, entertainment—art galleries, craft societies, designers, prospective authors, meaningful publishing companies, enterprising individuals have a right to be considered for financial assistance by sensible governments, so it is essential that appropriate governmental agencies know what's what.

Importantly, governmental and philanthropic assessors of projects must be visionary, knowledgeable, canny, sympathetic and, at the same time, tough—for there are shysters out there. The funders must at all times be available! Public servants are just that, servants of the public, paid by the public. A tendency in 'business' nowadays seems to be a concentration on unavailability, on rebuttal—he/she's 'at a meeting', 'in conference' or 'attending such and such' but unavailable. Rarely is one invited to 'ring me on this number' or 'send me an email to this address'. Too often one is directed to a website, or negated by a minder whose job it is to 'repel morons'. Bring back the one-on-one technique. Where is Brian Epstein when we need him?

18 Health and Education

If we get The President's and First Australian Academies up, I feel sure that Australia will be guided, wisely, into best possible health and education standards and policies, to establish us as a nation to lead the world. Indeed, health and education are the two principal areas of social wellbeing. If we are unwell and/or uneducated, we are 'up Schipp Creek without a paddle' as the wonderful TV commercial tells us.

In education, we would be well-advised to start by referring back to age old societal lifestyles, where grandparents especially had a role to play. There was once no official childcare and the oldies enjoyed their participation in bringing up the youngies.

> The most important requirement in a child's development is love; that takes plenty of meaningful time, enabling children to acquire wisdom and good habits.

The most important requirement in a child's development is love; that takes plenty of meaningful time, enabling children to acquire wisdom and good habits. Nowadays, most young families need two parental incomes and necessarily seek Childcare assistance as a right. Yes, Childcare should be available, free, at all times, for all families; while rigorous standards in that quarter must be maintained, surely we could somehow subsidise grandparents or other rellies to help out, or somehow get involved?

I loved the astute comment by eminent anthropologist Margaret Mead, when asked by Robert Moore on ABCTV: "You mention wonderful relationships with your grandchildren, Margaret. How come?' She replied: 'Well, we have a common enemy'.

The same ABCTV recently had a lovely program, where children from Childcare Centres visited Old Timers Homes. The outcome was delightful. 'Come on, Reg, smarten up', said the four year old, as she took compliant 84 year old Reg to tour the garden. The two groups need and generally relate to one another. Can we do more of this sort of thing at policy level? Create these centres as adjoining properties? On a concerted, deliberate national basis?

Education to the ultimate level is a universal right in democratic society and should never be determined by uneven distribution of wealth. Secular education must be available for all and highest basic standards must be set—and met. People have every right to run independent schools; let them charge whatever fees their followers are happy to pay; good luck to them. But they should never be subsidised at a level above *the norm*.

I suggested earlier that there should be more encouragement for children to progress through primary school, on to Trade Schools and Hospitality Training Schools, but let's forget the old-fashioned gender biases. It is a different world. No pinks and blues, we're all green for 'Go', for 'Ready, Set ... 'Kutju'.

University education is presently achievable on the basis of scholastic attainment at appropriate level. Let's keep those standards high, let us aim for the ultimate, for we are going to be world leaders. But, once attained, via monumental endeavour, university study should be free for all. Calculating and recouping HECS loans is not the way to go. We want achievers and we want them achieving, for the benefit of the nation. A fair investment, via Students Allowance payments, will in most cases be repaid abundantly in the ensuing lives of graduates in their chosen fields. A substantial bonus for graduates to work in regional and remote regions?

Schools need teachers of the highest quality. Some countries—Finland and Canada for two—have established an admirable standard of all round educational excellence. Let us examine how they did it.

Let us not be afraid to try different tactics. As an example, I trained to be a teacher much later than most, in my early 30s. Most of my fellow trainees at Teachers College were 18–19 year olds, matriculants all, eager to learn but quite immature in many cases. I certainly don't claim to have had a better experience than the younger students—many of them went on to illustrious careers—but with children of my own I knew what I wanted. I was painfully aware of the shortcomings in my own education. I also was aware that I was training for the specific task of one-teacher education for First Australian children. So I was able to take some of the more adventurous lecturers into my individual differences and requirements.

At the same time, my father Joe Egan was over 70; I remain certain that he would have made an ideal school teacher, at that age. The paradox was that he did not have the educational standard to qualify: his own schooling had ended at Grade 4, when he was required to leave school and work on the family farm. As a self-taught adult he had acquired literary skills and a level of knowledge that would have been the envy of many academics, especially in the political arena. Joe had survived the Depression of the 1930s, raised five of his own children in an environment of love, laughter, self-discipline, family unity, music. Yes, we were poor, but each of our five siblings went on to a lifetime of achievement.

> **Joe had survived the Depression of the 1930s, raised five of his own children in an environment of love, laughter, self-discipline, family unity, music.**

On many occasions, I saw my dear old Dad surrounded by 30 of his grandchildren, all together. Every one of them attests, today, to the wonderful influence their grandfather had, introducing songs, tricks, basic wisdom and a ton of fun into their developing lives. They sat at his feet and adored him. In a different manner—my Mum, Grace, who was often a perfect foil for Joe. Mind you, Grace was known as 'the Nana with the looking face'; only two of her grandchildren ever 'took her on'. I can testify to her forthrightness!

So, how about training courses for prospective teachers, at any age?

In the Covid era, we are experiencing many situations where education of our children has to be undertaken 'at home'. I think we will be doing this for years, perhaps forever. I have always advocated that the principles established in Australia around one-teacher schools and School of the Air, nowadays called Distance Education, can be modified and applied in all forms of education. We now have the 'online' techniques that can examine these established techniques and positively connect to present day circumstances and requirements.

> In the Covid era, we are experiencing many situations where education of our children has to be undertaken 'at home.' I think we will be doing this for years, perhaps forever.

The results speak for themselves. In one-teacher schools, children learn to solve their own problems; there are no discipline issues. The teacher plans lessons in such a manner that he or she works exclusively with one group of kids, while at all times older kids are supervising a younger group. At Newcastle Waters in the 1960s I had 24 pupils, including three of my own. It was immense fun; we achieved at every level. Importantly, the First Australian parents of the kids from the nearby cattle station were so impressed that they asked for adult-education lessons. They taught me so much! And I have never been so exhausted.

Distance Education caters for children in remote regions, sometimes 500 km from their teachers in town. Nowadays the contact is eye to eye, on computer screens. At the outset it was done via pedal radio and the mailing of voluminous correspondence lessons between bush kids and supervisors. Today, the principles are the same. Each child is treated as an individual. A program is laid out. The children accept responsibility at a surprising level in most cases. There is a need for an adult supervisor, principally as a guide and co-ordinator. This is sometimes a parent, in some cases a governess, occasionally a VISE mentor.

I was Patron of VISE—Volunteers for Isolated Students Education—for many years. VISE was founded by a magnificent visionary named Mike Stock; today it is supported by Aussie Helpers, led by Brian and Nerida Egan (not closely related as far as I know, but similar Celtic origins).

The members of VISE—retired teachers, many from former top echelon posts—volunteer to assist bush families, in times of crisis or need, with the education of children whose school is 'in the home', usually in very remote circumstances.

It is a wonderful enterprise, totally independent of government funding. Volunteer teachers are of individual means; they work for no payment, but their basic travelling costs are covered by VISE.

Let's say Mum, who lives out bush with her family, is due to have her fourth child. She is required to be 'away from home' for a period and is certainly going to need help around the school lessons of her other three kids on the station or farm. The VISE volunteer arrives. The kids get the bonus, the expertise of a retired teacher who may formerly have been Principal of some toffy city college. The Volunteer is usually impressed by the positive lifestyle of country people. I have heard volunteers refer to their sojourns as 'staycations'. Not unexpectedly, the word gets around. It is called 'the bush telegraph'. 'When that volunteer finishes at yours, can he/she come to us?' goes on the network: a win/win situation is the anticipated outcome: it's called mateship. The children benefit. Lives change.

Let us seek ways to incorporate our oldies in the teaching process, rather than look for reasons to put them into Aged Homes. And let us at all times make school so exciting that the word 'compulsory' never crosses our minds.

Health Matters Generally

In health, we simply want the best possible outcome for all of our people, regardless of the cost. Government invariably acknowledges its responsibility through Medicare, but does not always deliver the goods. Wealthier people may participate in expensive medical benefit funds, but adequate treatment must be there for every citizen at all times and in all places. Ill health compounds issues, bringing with it low morale, depression, neglect, mental health issues and suicides. Massive funding is needed, but it is a negative economic approach that we create. Let's have some positive thinking to create a healthy, vigorous society.

We have, in most cases in Australia, access to a medical system that should make us all superfolk. Generally our hospitals, medical centres, ambulance services, medical practitioners, physios, chiropractors, remedial centres and nurses, are top level. Many services are free; where payment is required it is usually deemed reasonable. We keep telling one another that 'we live in the luckiest country in the world' and that is a fair appraisal of Australia—certainly in medical matters, for most—but not all of our people, unfortunately.

> ... we are overweight, most of us are not physically fit, we are prone to diabetes, kidney failure, heart issues, we drink too many sugary drinks and too much alcohol.

The dilemma is that statistics tell us we are on a general downward curve. On a national level, we are overweight, most of us are not physically fit, we are prone to diabetes, kidney failure, heart issues, we drink too many sugary drinks and too much alcohol. Many of us are addicted to drugs, especially tobacco. Australia is perhaps the 'ice capital' of the world.

Mental health is a huge issue nowadays. In my childhood, people with obvious mental problems were committed to asylums dubbed 'loony bins' where they were locked in cells, subjected to cruel, often criminal disciplines, erratic medication; they were often 'restrained' by devices like 'straight jackets'. Then the policy changed, the asylums were closed and families were expected to care for and cope with their own affected, suffering members.

That would have been commendable if benign intent was accompanied by determined research into the cause of the various levels of damage, a concentration on developing medication at appropriate levels and a comprehensive, regular check on all known cases.

As happens so often in Australia because of our bewildering Constitution, there was never a national standard set. Was mental health a State or a Federal responsibility? To this day it is a vexed question, highlighted by too many instances of seemingly inexplicable, incomprehensible violence, followed by bewildered exchanges of acronyms and expressions of regret. Such is the wisdom of hindsight: it is not good enough to know that 'it was bound to happen'.

There is an obvious requirement to recognise danger early, to create a system that enables patients and their families to get prompt, effective medical treatment in times of crisis, to have all sections of society better educated about ominous signs. Suicide—too often an outcome of perplexed mental suffering—is devastating for all parties involved; it is a sad paradox that to my knowledge—there is no word in any First Australian language that translates as 'the taking of one's own life'. Once inconceivable, because of inbuilt kinship responsibilities, it is now a scourge among First Australians, especially the young innocents.

Wonderful organisations like *Lifeline* and *Beyond Blue* must be supported appropriately, enabled to set world standards in recognition and prevention.

The essential elements of a healthy society are:

- good diet
- sufficient exercise
- positive attitude to life in general
- respect for all of our fellow humans
- moderation in all habits
- a preparedness to assist others
- respect for the medical experts, doctors, nurses
- comfortable housing and lifestyle for all citizens
- possession of the means to enable a good life
- modesty, in mind and body.

The old Latin adage: *mens sana in corpore sano* sums it up. A sound mind in a healthy body.

The ball is largely within the court of we players. The role of government is to keep the standards high.

19 The Health of First Australians

The 'Gap' that currently exists for First Australian societies in all matters is simply not tolerable; as Winston Churchill was wont to say, 'It is a situation, up with which we will not put'. The Gap applies in all aspects of life, but in my opinion the entire state of inequality derives from ill health, brought on by mal-nourishment. Usually there is just not enough food. Additionally, the quality of available foodstuffs is inferior. Diet is the area that needs to be remedied, over and above all the other shortcomings and disadvantages.

We are constantly told the dreadful statistics. First Australians are undoubtedly the unhealthiest people in Australia. Afflictions like diabetes, heart issues, kidney failure are commonplace, eye and ear troubles are a problem for the majority. Name the disease or illness, they suffer from it. Life expectancy is well below the average of other societal groups. Although some valuable work is constantly being performed in various quarters and there is undoubtedly an impressive body of health workers dedicated to doing the necessary tasks, we seem to be going backwards.

> **First Australians are undoubtedly the unhealthiest people in Australia.**

We only need to examine our history to find out why.

In the process of dispossession, we took over their lives, we ruined their diet, we refused to learn clever things from them, we separated them from traditional foodstuffs and methods of living 'off the land'. We denied and betrayed their very existence.

Nowadays First Australians are in constant attendance at hospitals. Yes, there are many very dedicated doctors, nurses and hospital staff who do a sterling job trying to cope, but it is basically hopeless. There are language issues, cultural problems galore. A huge factor is that if an old person gets sick out bush, an entire family will (of course) see the need to accompany the invalid to hospital. So a patient at hospital may be accompanied by ten family members, who are required to forsake all else. There is no other option. That is how family works. Sadly, the entire family structure is endangered at that point.

While the kinship system that First Australians developed during countless centuries of a satisfactory lifestyle was totally appropriate pre-1788, it is a huge problem in the everyday life imposed on them via colonialism. They have attitudes and expectations that western society will not tolerate. Albert Namatjira was a case in point. I knew Albert very well and admired everything about him. He was a very handsome, dignified man, a celebrated artist. I wrote a song about him:

> When I was young I walked this land
> With wise old men who said:
> 'When we change you to a man,
> If you don't share, you're dead!'

He was given 'citizenship' by the new system, because by western standards he was such an impressive achiever. The same system subsequently gaoled him for sharing a bottle of wine with his sons. Albert died a very deluded man. Valé.

Some factual background may help younger readers understand the complexity of it all. The impact of First Australian ill-health is staggering and I watch, so saddened, because I know how it happened. They identify with their kinfolk even though they are aware they have been dispossessed, demoralised, deprived. There is a very privileged elite among them, but First Australians are generally impoverished.

The majority of First Australians live in unsatisfactory accommodation, where basic quality foodstuffs are either not available or are of lesser standard, invariably at exorbitant prices. Add all those factors together. That state of demoralisation affects the entire lifestyle. I am aware how difficult it will be to effect change. Our system has done them no favours. I have heard all the high faluting theories over many years. I live in Alice Springs, at the heart of this dilemma; I don't want to hear theories. At age 89, I want to know why so many of my First Australian friends died so young, why 19 out of 20 wheelchairs carry Aboriginal invalids.

Historic Background

Post about 1800, when it was obvious that the British were in Australia to stay, emancipist convicts and a few soldier settlers were 'granted' tracts of land. Then, ominously, wealthier free citizens from Britain began to take up offers of huge tracts of 'Crown' land—often sight unseen. Arbitrary lines were drawn on maps 12,000 miles away—for the continent of Australia was deemed *terra nullius*.

Much has been written about the 'resistance fighters' like Pemulwuy, near Sydney; Yagan, near Perth; later Tjandamara in the Kimberley and other warriors who recognised the intentions of the 'invaders' and took them on. Spear throwers had no chance against gun shooters on horseback, so the results generally were predictable. Although there was, in a few regions, stalwart opposition from the original owners, in skirmishes nowadays referred to as 'frontier wars', the statistics tell that they were generally one-sided conquests.

The most damaging aspect of the takeover by the new 'owners' of the various regions at all times was the deviousness of it all. A total new lifestyle was imposed on First Australians, invariably against their best interests, presented under the guise of protection, when it was always about exploitation. Today there is a demand for Truth Telling, comparable to the process introduced to post-apartheid South Africa by Nelson Mandela and Archbishop Desmond Tutu. So here is a framework, around which individual stories need to be recorded. But keep in mind that we are talking about a system imposed on people who had lived in harmony with the same country for thousands of generations, people who knew this country inside out.

The Five Stages of Dispossession.

Period 1

Our history records the first tokenistic attempts at amelioration—the mirrors, axes, necklaces, blankets and bags of flour. Batman's Treaty etc. The blatant bribes.

Period 2

When that period soured, more direct tactics were implemented. The gifts: the odd poisoned bag of flour. Or pink (strychnine-laced) sugar. Take it or leave it, Jacky. Whitefellas are here for keeps. Work for us in menial tasks on our terms; stop killing our cattle and sheep, or we'll get rid of you. 'The Martini Henry speaks English', said the monstrous Constable Willshire of his Winchester rifle.

> **The gifts: the odd poisoned bag of flour. Or pink (strychnine-laced) sugar. Take it or leave it, Jacky.**

Period 3

That uncompromising stance by white authorities was reinforced by the very obvious reprisals and subsequent massacres that took place throughout the land—despite present-day protestations to the contrary. The last government-sponsored massacre of First Australians was at Coniston, Northern Territory, in 1928, when an acknowledged 31 men, women and children were shot dead by Constable Murray and his team of willing helpers, as reprisal for the murder of a derelict white man named Fred Brooks. The actual figure was certainly much higher, more likely 80–100. Teach the blacks a lesson.

Period 4

So the do-gooders asked: What do we do with the remnants of Aboriginal society? The best means of dispossession was to get them off the good lands, take them to concentration camps—usually called 'mission stations'—where they were subject to proselytism, inferior diet and the unhealthy admixture of people of different clans, who had wisely avoided contact with one another for countless centuries.

Rogues like Baldwin Spencer, appointed to Chief Protector status, kept telling the First Australians that we were there to protect them, to help them to a better life. God was on our side of course, represented by pictures of a daunting old white man with a flowing beard. But we denied them good diets in almost all of our dealings. It can only be described as sinister, criminal.

> **We specifically disfranchised them. No, you can't vote, you're not civilised. They were not on the national census, for they were considered to be a sub-species.**

We specifically disfranchised them. No, you can't vote, you're not civilised. They were not on the national census, for they were considered to be a sub-species. 'Aboriginal natives of Australia shall not be counted' was written into the 1901 Constitution.

Yet nobody was more specifically kept 'on record'. Throughout Australia, there were Mission Boards or somesuch, where extensive individual records were kept of every First Australian person, in order that they could be kept 'under control'; so that the full level of discrimination ('protection') could be exercised against them. Nobody else in Australia was 'counted' so often, but always for the wrong reasons. In my early years as a Patrol Officer, we conducted a detailed Census everywhere we went. We guessed at dates of birth and these were registered on the appropriate individual files.

There was invariably legislation, at State, Territory or local government level, based on race. Aboriginals were subject to the whim of The Chief Protector or whatever title was in vogue. First Australians were required to live on reserves, they were not allowed to be in 'white' towns between sunset and sunrise, they were subject to 'committal' to various penal establishments if they stepped out of line. They were required to work wherever they were placed and their employers were required to have licences. Their wages (if any) were not paid direct to them; usually the so called 'wage' was considerably lower than for other employees and a percentage was deducted for food—always referred to as 'rations', always basic foodstuffs, usually of poor quality.

Tribal people in some regions were still able to live off the land, but then further devious tactics were devised in order to retain control for government employees or missionaries. Schooling was compulsory, so it became appropriate to build dormitories, to enable children to be separated from 'pagan' or 'primitive' parents.

Inferior food for an entire race was the 'norm' for otherwise-affluent Australia. Inferior food causes ill-health more than anything else. If you are mal-nourished you are vulnerable to every germ, every sickness, every virus; you are physically weak, prone to injury. Combine that with financial poverty, overcrowding in unhygienic accommodation and disruption of traditional family life via all the forms of discrimination that were exercised. What else could we expect but the present chasm that we call 'the gap'?

No wonder eminent First Australian poet and playwright Jack Davis wrote these poignant lines:

> No sugar in our tea
> Bread and butter we never see
> That's why we're gradually
> Fading away.

Readers are urged to study Jack's fine works.

Crucial to that era was the discouragement of traditional practices and stamping out old Australian languages. Culture? What culture, asked our community leaders?

Period 5

Those Aboriginals who did not fit into mission life, for whatever reason, drifted to the edges of towns, where generation after generation followed the same paths as their unfortunate ancestors. It was quickly established by the newcomers that there was a propensity, among the original owners of the now appropriated land, for addiction to substances like alcohol, tobacco, opium and hard cash, so women were traded for sexual congress. It was assumed that First Australians of the full descent would die out. 'Fuck them white' was a term often expressed by the white men involved.

Institutions were established where girls of mixed race were trained for domestic service, boys as stock workers and farm labourers. It was proposed that, thereby, they would eventually be 'bred white'. The original owners of regions became powerless fringe dwellers in their own country, always subject to discrimination, always at the rear of the queue. The question of land ownership was thereby resolved in the minds of the latterday colonists. The original First Australians had not totally disappeared—as people had anticipated—but nobody was going to take them seriously when they protested that their land had been stolen from them. Many became addicted to things addictive, they were easily dismissed. Forgotten.

Period 6

Sadly, in the 1950s the question of 'identity' prompted a divisive move among many First Australians of mixed descent. They sought different, indeed preferential treatment from that exercised against their relations known as 'full bloods'. Particularly in the Northern Territory there was a tendency for mixed race individuals to identify with the non-Aboriginal component of their heritage: people insisted that they were Malays, Filipinos, Chinese, or whatever, in order to seek exemption from the Aboriginals Ordinance. It was not vindictive, but they were encouraged to identify thus, with certain social and financial opportunities offered accordingly. Xavier Herbert's book *Capricornia* covers the subject perceptively: 'I'm a Malay prince' insisted Norman (Nawnim = No name). Bodies with contentious names like the AHPA (Australian Halfcastes Progress Association) and the Eurabo League were formed, successfully leading to the passage of the Welfare Ordinance in 1954, whereby all people of mixed Aboriginal race were given freedom.

They were indeed confused times. Contemporaneously, Paul Hasluck, as a wily Minister for Territories, was aware of international recrimination against Australia over its treatment of Aboriginal people. Fiji, Singapore and South Africa led the onslaught, although South Africa modelled its *apartheid* policy on Australia, as it too sought to declare Blacks and Coloureds as sub-species. Paul Hasluck was subsequently criticised for co-operating with the AHPA. There is no doubt that the much-maligned Hasluck actively supported the members of that group; he established firm and staunch friendships in the process.

I was present in 1953—sharing an upstairs office in Darwin at the old NT Administration in Cavenagh Street—when Hasluck personally dictated the terms of the new Welfare Ordinance to a man named Jack Huthnance, who spent the next six months drafting the legislation. I am a good listener, thanks to my Mum.

The specific aim of the new legislation was that Australia, within its federally run Northern Territory, was eliminating laws based on race—a specific race, the Australian Aboriginals. The Commonwealth had no race powers in any of the six States, which Constitutionally since 1901 had been the preserve of the various State governments, all of which had similar, even more discriminatory powers than those prevailing in the NT.

The new NT Welfare Ordinance of 1954 effectively terminated the old 1918 NT Aboriginals Ordinance, implemented in 1912 by Baldwin Spencer, which purported to 'protect' Aboriginals but in fact had discriminated against them solely on the basis of race. Now the same set of discriminatory laws were implemented, but on the basis of 'need'. Persons in need because of their 'inability without assistance adequately to manage their own affairs' were to be declared to be Wards of the Director of Welfare. On a given day, 15,439 'full blood' Aboriginals were declared to be 'Wards'. On that same day, the Director of Native Affairs was named the Director of Welfare. Only a handful of mixed race

> On a given day, 15,439 'full blood' Aboriginals were declared to be 'Wards'.

persons were deemed to be 'in need'. A rose by yet another name was still a blackfella. The book listing the names and locations of 'the wards' came—irreverently—to be known as 'The Stud Book'. Racist 'jokes' abounded.

As an outcome of exploitative miscegenation, the skin colour of most First Australians paled, the traditional languages were lost and they were encouraged to 'live like whites'—but always on the edges of white society. The 'whiteness' did not stop the discrimination. Pejorative words like 'half-castes', 'yellerfellers' were used as identifiers of people who 'had a touch of the tar brush', in much the same way as Jews were forced to wear a yellow Star of David by the Nazis. It was decreed in Australia that the embarrassing, mixed race children would be removed from 'undesirable circumstances'. 'Out of sight, out of mind', said their white fathers. We now refer to them as 'The Stolen Generation'.

> **A rose by yet another name was still a blackfella. The book listing the names and locations of 'the wards' came — irreverently — to be known as 'The Stud Book.' Racist 'jokes' abounded.**

Period 7

But then we had the establishment of FCAATSI (Federal Council for the Advancement of Aboriginals and Torres Strait Islanders), the 1963 Bark Petition, the Gurindji walkoff, the 'land rights' demos of the 1960s, the 1967 Referendum, the Whitlam election slogan: *It's Time*; the Woodward Royal Commission, Mabo, Wik and the subsequent, admirable declarations (like Paul Keating's Redfern Address*)* that traditional ownership of the land could be recognised, wherever there was evidence that traditional practices and associations were still in existence. It came to be called 'land rights' and tokenistic pieces of paper were distributed. *Welcome to Country* speeches were delivered, 'smoking' ceremonies were enacted. A Reconciliation Council was appointed. 'Sorry Books' were implemented and the 'Stolen Generation' was apologised for, but without financial compensation. 'Truth Telling'—an Australian version of the 'Truth and Reconciliation' process in South Africa *post apartheid*—is proposed. I support that move; I am very willing to participate. Hope for the future.

Personal Reminiscence: Truth Telling

I have lived through Periods four, five, six and seven (above). We who derive from Europe and other Continents imposed a dreadful change of lifestyle on the First Australians; we must seek and endorse amendments. I find it hard to use the word '*re*-conciliation', even though I was privileged by my appointment to the First Reconciliation Council. 'When did we have "conciliation"?' I asked. Let us seek *Recognition*, with people like me seeking to identify what went wrong.

I'll start with a single sentence. Our principal crime was to impose on most First Australians an inferior diet, as a component tactic of dispossession. I submit that that sentence explains more than anything else the cause for all the 'worst in Australia' statistics—longevity, health, education, disability, alcohol and drug addiction, criminal activity, incarceration, recidivism. I propose that there be a survey asking: 'What is the detail of your diet this week?' to every First Australian. I wager that the outcome will show that, even today, the overwhelming majority of First Australians are mal-nourished. They survive on tea, bread or damper, Johnny cakes and gravy, chips and tomato sauce, hot dogs, the occasional KFC or Maccas. Liquid intake? Tea—loaded with sugar—Coke, Fanta, beer, cheap wine, strong spirits.

In a career spanning 25 years with first Northern Territory Native Affairs, then Department of Aboriginal Affairs, I spent the years 1958–1963 as Superintendent at Yuendumu—290 km north-west of Alice Springs—a government 'settlement', as such places were called in those 'post—mission and pre-community' times. All such titles are euphemisms for 'camp' or 'ration centre', rather than 'normal township'.

That is how Australia 'handled its blackfellas' when they were removed from the better lands. They were to be given menial issues of flour, tea, sugar—and tobacco! It was deemed 'their *right*'. There was an occasional tin of meat, perhaps a 'bonus' tin of jam or Golden Syrup, known as Bullockies Joy. Ernie Dingo recorded my song '*Bullockies Joy and*

Jesus'—relating to a mission station that issued a tin of Golden Syrup on 'ration day' to those who had attended church often enough to qualify. Once a year, women received a dress, men were given trousers and shirts, all adults got a blanket at Christmas. Kids were issued clean clothes at school each day; they had a shower and a reasonable lunch of stew. Maximum wage was £2 a week for men, £1 a week for women. Bank notes were often held together by skilful sewing, impaired by constant use and re-use at the 'store', where luxuries like tins of fruit could be purchased.

At the commencement of my time at Yuendumu, there were no houses whatsoever for the 1000 Warlpiri residents—survivors of the deplorable Coniston Massacre, they were now 'relocated' at Yuendumu. The congregated Warlpiri lived in 'humpies'—'tjitabyan' (sheet of iron) became the operative word—around the minimal administrative buildings: four houses for white staff, a ration store, a small communal kitchen, a small hospital, sometimes with two nurses but occasionally none, a good quality pre-school and primary school that produced some outstanding First Australian pupils.

The Warlpiri were just so tough. All wore clothing during the day; most stripped naked to sleep on the bare ground at night, in temperatures as low as minus 5° Celsius in winter months. Small fire, body, small fire, body, the occasional dog.

Ceremonial life was still very strict, very strong. Everybody—including all whites—observed local kinship and avoidance rules, which were articulated clearly and profoundly by appropriate elders. School attendance: 100%

In those days all Yuendumu babies were born in bush camps, delivered by expert midwives who had the knowledge; more importantly, they also knew the correct songs and ceremonies. I do not recall one complicated birth situation in five years. There was no alcohol, so today's curse of foetal alcohol syndrome was unheard of.

Today in Central Australia all babies are 'required' to be born in hospitals. Where are these hospitals? Only in the big towns: Alice Springs for the mothers of Yuendumu. Prime Minister, let us build those Bob Beadman towns, empower the local First Australian residents, enable them to negotiate to hire the best quality doctors and nurses, on their terms, as well as enjoying the skills of their own trainees in these fields. It is good economics, if nothing else.

I must acknowledge a sad statistic from the same Yuendumu, in the same era. I can attest that not one baby born in 1957 survived beyond twelve months. Probably 30 to 40 deaths. Why? Gastro enteritis. Most babies absolutely thrived to weaning age, for Warlpiri women are good mothers; problems ensued when the babies needed solid foods. My own children, living in the same region, went through the same stages, being carefully introduced to the standard baby foods, but these were not available to First Australian mothers.

> ... not one baby born in 1957 survived beyond twelve months.

I blamed the many deaths largely on the presence of dogs, who often accessed billy cans containing the same food and liquid given to babies. I became (and am still) paranoid about 'camp dogs'. I shot hundreds, but made no impact on the scourge. This old white paternalist can only plead for all traditional First Australians to do some important things:

- stop sitting on the ground
- get rid of dogs in your lives
- eat better foods
- face up to the cultural and health dilemmas surrounding alcohol and drugs.

I remain pensive about my past; I reminisce, realising that I was a contributor in a system where the will of the white man was pre-determined to prevail. I was first appointed as a *Protector of Aborigines* in 1952 by the much-maligned Sir Paul Hasluck, whose role in Aboriginal Affairs is completely misunderstood. His major concern in life was a better deal for First Australians and his coining of the phrase 'assimilation' outlined his determination that all Australians should be able to access a worthy lifestyle. I was then and remain steadfastly today, determined to seek to do positive things to rectify the injustices perpetrated against First Australians. I must acknowledge that I was then and remain, a paternalist. I was mentored by some wonderful men and women, including Aboriginals and people of many other races and backgrounds. I always have been and always will be 'on the side' of First Australians in matters of land and identity, but when I was appointed as the youngest ever Superintendent of an Aboriginal Reserve, I acknowledge that I was too imbued with the Western work ethic. I should have concentrated on sitting down with knowledgeable elders, to learn how better to handle the new, imposed lifestyle. We surely could have managed important matters like the above dog question better? I sought to impose a 'Let's have no dogs' policy. The locals said 'We need dogs for hunting'. I had the key of the ration store, so my will prevailed at all times. I should have sought a better, workable solution.

I am proud that the Warlpiri of Yuendumu had quite a reputation in those days as 'achievers'. We ran a successful cattle station, managed by skilful, experienced old Warlpiri men. Our best team of labourers were elderly, strong, fun-loving women. Unload the supply truck? 'Stand back and watch us, fellers!' Those same women once collected a huge shipment of mulga seed—*acacia aneura*—which we sold to the United Nations, netting the women a financial result they could not believe, £50 dollars each, a year's wages for collecting bush tucker!

We always ensured reasonable supply of protein for all people, either through our own beef—four 'killers' a week—or through regular organised, skilful shooting of kangaroos, usually twenty a week at least. We had prize-winning market gardens, showed initiative in simple house construction, using local materials and local labour, had an awesome reputation in Aussie Rules football. Sadly—how often I use that word nowadays—there is no lasting Yuendumu legacy today, other than in footy.

> We always ensured reasonable supply of protein for all people, either through our own beef—four 'killers' a week—or through regular organised, skilful shooting of kangaroos, usually twenty a week at least.

I must take some of the blame for today's outcomes. I eventually advanced to Level One public servant status and always felt positive, endorsing ideas like the Bob Beadman towns. But my friend—First Australian spokeswoman Pat Turner—is right when she says: 'My people once ran this country effectively. It's time to give us room again, to enable us to work—and I mean work—out our own destiny. It won't be easy and we will need compassion and assistance'.

    I seek the same approach for all of Australia. Build up the regions, reduce the importance of the capital cities, use our wonderful assets for the benefit of all of our people. Let's work together at all times.

20 The Education of First Australians

Normally I deplore use of the past tense in respect of First Australians, such as we were taught in schools in Australia when I was a child, e.g., 'The aborigines (with a lower case *a*) *were* primitive people. They *lived* in bark humpies and *hunted* kangaroos for their food'. We were led to believe that they once were numerous, but a sub-species, on the way to disappearance.

I wish to take the reader back to the times prior to 1787, to discuss traditional education among First Australians as the forerunner to the types of educative policies that have been imposed on them in subsequent years.

Traditionally, First Australians were born into highly regulated societies, where no question was unanswerable among those recognised as possessors of 'the knowledge'. It was crucial to realise that every form of Nature had a place in the overall perspectives of the group—call it tribe, clan, nation, whatever term appeals to you. People were accorded 'totems' that prescribed certain affinities, behaviour and attitudes towards birds, animals, plants, as well as fellow human beings. Basically, an individual's identity derived from the mother, for there was no denying who she was; an inheritance to land derived from the father and was usually based on patrilineal descent lines.

There is a tendency nowadays among First Australians of mixed descent to over-identify. One hears people say: 'I am Gurindji and Larakia on my father's side, Wiradjuri and Yorta Yorta on my mother's side'. This is obviously an admirable desire to achieve optimum solidarity, but it also indicates a lack of real understanding concerning inheritance. And it is often used as a denial of any DNA factors other than Aboriginal.

> Children are taught to respect their precious mainstay, their country. They do not own the land: the land is always the dominant factor in the lives of the people.

Traditionally, children are allowed to be uninhibited, to learn by experience, in the knowledge that the elders know the ropes and will oversee the hunting and gathering practices, the appurtenant ceremonial observations, the future moves to be made in what is still unique harmony with Nature. All necessities are available as long as the proper behavioural patterns are followed. They were not farmers as some writers would have us believe; they are logical beneficiaries of a bountiful Nature in a temperate land. Children are taught to respect their precious mainstay, their country. They do not own the land: the land is always the dominant factor in the lives of the people.

At a certain age—which varies, depending on the harshness of the country—children are slowly and deliberately prepared for initiation into the various levels of adulthood. They join small groups where specific adults teach appropriate songs, dances and ceremonies to enable an understanding of Nature and its benefits. It is all very jolly and full of fun in bountiful areas, but serious and much more secret in arid lands.

Along the way, the kinship system is drilled into the children: this is the complex detail of your birth and inheritance; these are the people who will look after you; these are the people you avoid in most circumstances; these are the likely partners for you in eventual parenthood; these are the people with whom you have nil contact. Sing these songs to implant in your mind what is required of you when you get older. This is the way you defend yourself if combat eventuates.

Children become knowledgeable, competent hunters and gatherers at around age seven years, required to learn all the appropriate practices in food gathering and use of artifacts required for effective hunting. Tracking is usually taught by old women. There were traditionally no books or charts—nowadays in some regions there are very good written works—but rote learning of songs imparts skills and proper techniques for respecting the land and the environment.

The next stage is physical initiation, where children are isolated from their families into the care of designated elders, to learn the more intricate stages of approaching adulthood. Degrees of secrecy concerning imparted knowledge are explained, penalties for lack of conformity are stressed. Comprehensive body painting is usually a concomitant factor, followed by a ceremonial return to society as 'initiates', henceforth recognised as responsible adults. Physical maturation procedures follow, like circumcision for most males, followed by sub-incision in harsher regions. Traditionally scarification was in vogue for both males and females, front tooth excision in some regions, until full adulthood was achieved. Initiation ceremonies were similar but varied in mainland tribes: a notable exception was the Tiwi people of north Australia, who do not practice circumcision, have very unique ceremonies, but also encouraged (extensively in earlier days) very intricate body scarification, totally different from all other groups. It is fair to say that the Tiwi had a stronger level of gender equality than any other group in Australia.

It was—and is still in a few regions—a very sensible educative process, in that it enabled all people to have a total knowledge of their environment that would enable a harmonious life to be lived. Yes there was occasional friction but most groups developed strict rules for fighting, like the stone knife duels of Central Australia, the makarrta trial by ordeal of Arnhem Land. Total 'warfare' as in other societies was rarely contemplated: people were too precious, the land had to be cared for. There were appeasement ceremonies to prevent such disasters.

> **Children become knowledgeable, competent hunters and gatherers at around age seven years**

And then in 1788 the colonisers arrived, quickly asserting that they had taken over a *terra nullius*, for they perceived no local signs of civilisation in their Western eyes. The new settlers were aware, of course, of the prior presence in Australia of a different race of black-skinned people, but it was easy to write that group off as a sub-species. The word quickly spread among the whites that, if the right cards were played, this embarrassing group would eventually disappear, either unable to handle introduced sicknesses, organised massacres, or via the process of miscegenation: fucking them white.

But they did not disappear. Efforts were then made by white governmental authorities to separate the children from 'cruel tribal practices' and give them a Western education that would hopefully enable them to see the sense of being like whites. Because First Australians had quickly come to realise that white people enjoyed endorsement of their policies, the strange new educative practice was generally accepted as 'a good idea'. In some areas very favourable results were achieved and a sense of scholarship developed. There was no contemplation of an educated elite however, as the total lifestyle of Aboriginal groups was still considered 'primitive'.

Christian missionaries were invited by various governments to run the concentration camps called missions. Proselitism became the norm and again, many Aboriginals willingly and graciously accepted membership of the various Christian denominations. Some missions were better than others, measured (in my judgement) by the degree of intrusion into traditional, pre-1788 practices, particularly the use of old languages, polygyny and promised marriages. In the Northern Territory, where I have considerable experience, I am of the opinion that the Methodists in Arnhem Land were best, followed by Lutherans in Central Australia, Roman Catholics in both the Top End and the Centre; and CMS Anglicans in the Top End, in that order.

My reason for placing the Methodists first is that

they did not seek to insist on First Australians becoming Methodists; in fact they encouraged traditional ceremonies and use of local languages. I must pay tribute here to a remarkable woman, an enterprising young teacher named Beulah Lowe, who came to the Northern Territory in 1954, determined to learn local languages, hopeful of translating the Bible into those languages. Based at Milingimbi over the next twenty years Beulah not only achieved those targets, she also established an important principle. In gratitude to the adults who had taught her, she taught them to be literate themselves in their languages—in Arnhem Land referred to as Yolngu Matha—the language of the local people. As a consequence those proud, now literate adults inculcated in their own children the value of a good Western-style 'education' as a back up to the traditional knowledge acquired from the appropriate First Australian authorities. The outcome speaks for itself.

There are differing schools of thought in various Education Departments concerning the language question in schools that cater mainly for First Australian children. Some departmental heads deplore the use of traditional languages, considering it tokenistic at best. In many cases they are right. But there is no doubt in my mind that, in the few regions where traditional languages still have meaningful existence, the best possible approach is to train local First Australians as teachers; to include, as a component of that training, language laboratory sessions to enhance their literacy in their own languages. Thereby, we encourage a system where first language speakers of traditional languages are initially taught to be literate in their own languages, followed by a gradual concentration on spoken, written and reading skills in English. Children especially are capable of being literate in several languages at age 10.

To retain pride in their traditional societies it is essential that languages not only be retained, but studied, researched and learned by scholars around the world. Failure to do so will cause the eventual loss of the last surviving Australian languages, once numbering in the hundreds and arguably the oldest languages in world history. But let us establish a uniform orthography, one dependent solely on the 26 letter alphabet. No accents, no new keys on typewriters and word processors, please.

As my wife Nerys was born in Cymru (Wales), I am very aware of the success of the Welsh, who, despite 1500 years of colonialism comparable to Australia's experience, have retained their old language and culture. For most of that period the oppressors were English: throughout that period of abject linguistic persecution the Welsh preserved their own language, while the English language during the same period was slowly emerging in its own right. An interesting paradox to me is that educated Welsh people I know speak English better than the English!

> I propose that groups of educated First Australians competent in the languages of their ancestors be taken to Wales for study and research sessions ...

I propose that groups of educated First Australians competent in the languages of their ancestors be taken to Wales for study and research sessions, particularly concentrating on bi-lingual skills, in places like the Welsh Assembly, where the Welsh shine. There is a great need among First Australians for scholars able to speak, read and write both English and their traditional first language at academic level. There are very few First Australians of this status currently. I will be pleasantly surprised if there are 20 First Australians so endowed.

In this era when we seek to close the gap in so many areas concerning First Australians, there are invariably statistics indicating low attendance at schools. This won't be resolved by truancy officers, taxi services or fining parents. We must do what Beulah Lowe did: help adults to achieve literacy and indeed, other appurtenant skills, thereby engendering enthusiasm for schooling generally. I imagine that a First Australian Academy would very quickly concentrate on the need for appropriate educational curricula in traditional homelands, to enable the 1960s land rights objectives to be fulfilled. Schooling for children should then be conducted with concentration on the desirable dual lifestyle—traditional and Western—that will best serve all First Australians in these very different times. We should stop promoting objectives like 'compulsory education'; rather, make schooling so attractive that children insist on attending: it can happen.

21   Aged Care

Aged Care, better expressed as 'Care of the Aged' is a very vexed subject throughout Australia today. There has recently been a Royal Commission, following an ABC TV Four Corners program *Aged Care: Quality and Safety* in which it was revealed that there has been neglect, cruelty and mismanagement in the various centres that operate under the slogan: 'This is a home, not a hospital'.

Life is so different these days. We now discuss breast and prostate cancer at the dinner table. My dear friend Peter Lehmann used to say: 'OK, let's get the organ recital over first, before we got into our convivial drinks'. Mental health and dementia are a bit tougher to talk about. But shortcomings are on all of our minds, leading invariably to the dilemma for all seniors: home care or aged care?

Baby boomers (those born post 1945, all now heading for the last roundup) are wealthier, better informed and more demanding than were their own parents, so the nation must pay attention: We are Seniors and We Vote! Our politicians erred by initially providing huge assistance to the many profit-seekers who seized the commercial opportunity and established the first aged peoples' homes. At the outset, these institutions were for the privileged only, with emphasis on strict medical supervision. Admission rates were and still are exorbitant. Families of the elderly are in the Catch 22 position: we all have to work hard at our jobs in order to have the necessary cash flow to pay for the care of our parents, so again the query is: home care or aged care?

Gradually, as more and more families took the decision that they couldn't give Mum and Dad the care and attention that they needed, more and more centres for the aged were created. It was established—constitutionally—that the federal government was responsible for the funding of appropriate homes in the required regions. At the same time, State health departments were given the task of staffing the institutions. That created a deplorable dilemma. There was no national plan formulated for this vital issue, the care of our aged. Standards dropped and the staffing emphasis was on 'willing workers' rather than medical hotshots. Nursing is nowadays likely to be available only *in extremis*.

There was no planning whatsoever for a pandemic the level of Covid 19. We now know that a virus can sweep through premises occupied by vulnerable oldies. Management proved prone to panic. Let's close the gates, even barring relatives. Devastated families were denied access when Mum or Dad died. Not only are inmates affected: all staff members are equally vulnerable.

Let us hope that the findings of the subsequent royal commission provide the light that enables us to learn the appropriate lessons. Forget the home—or—hospital debate. We need the ideal combination, the best nursing staff and the kindest carers. The problem with royal commissions over the years, given our faulty three year election cycles, is that one government indignantly sets up the royal commission; too often, the next government fails to implement the proposed solutions. Fault is found with the preceding government that could not itself resolve the problem. The recommendations are often ignored. How many royal commissions have we had concerning bushfires?

The good health of our seniors is a top priority. We will all be old before we know it.

> **The good health of our seniors is a top priority. We will all be old before we know it.**

22 Attitudes to Gender

I AM SO GRATEFUL THAT I WAS BORN INTO A FAMILY THAT was strong concerning the respective roles of men and women—indeed females and males, to put them in alphabetical sequence, as required. The 'females and males' touch derives from my mother Grace, who insisted that alphabetical order must prevail in all things. She always said 'her or his'; she also sought 'gentlemen and ladies' for formal addresses. Gender was on her mind.

In the 1960s I took my mother to see the musical *South Pacific*. She enjoyed the outing, but deplored the attitudes portrayed on stage. In respect of the song 'There is Nothing Like a Dame', she said to me: 'Why can't men get their minds above their navels?' She hated all the slang terms tagged on to women, mainly on the grounds that there were no equivalent terms for men. 'Dame', 'Broad', 'Tart' etc. were invariably used pejoratively, indicating that women were lesser beings, there to be harassed, there for the pleasure and exploitative tactics of the dominant males.

I was raised in a family consisting of my Dad and Mum, three elder sisters, Pat (Patricia) Peg (Margaret) and Sal

(Shirley), me, then my younger brother Tim (Francis Geoffrey) born seven years later. Joe Egan, my Dad, had five sisters and two brothers. My Mum, Grace Brennan, had nine brothers and two sisters. All families of relatives had an unbringing similar to mine. You are equals as human beings, despite physical differences. You will respect and if necessary, protect one another. Most of our relatives were reared on farms by hard-working parents who demanded an equal contribution of physical hard work from each child.

My Mum taught me to wash and iron clothes and do household laundry and cleaning. I could mend holes in woollen socks, sew buttons on shirts at age ten, also cook simple basic meals. In my early years my three sisters taught me important things like tying shoelaces, telling the time, using scissors in the other hand. I read all of their books as well as those carefully chosen for me by my Dad, mostly concerning sporting heroes, female and male. I learned all the old-time dances as 'the requisite male partner' of my sisters; we all shared a love of music inherited from our parents. Grace usually suggested the songs to sing as we 'did the dishes' each evening. Such joy: we invariably prolonged the task to enjoy the songs.

> My Mum taught me to wash and iron clothes and do household laundry and cleaning ... Sadly, I was never taught 'the facts of life' by my parents ...

Sadly, I was never taught 'the facts of life' by my parents, but picked up scant knowledge from a few school mates. At the Christian Brothers College—boys only—we were simply told to respect, indeed revere all girls and women, who are 'created in the image of the Blessed Virgin Mary.' To this day, I support the principle of separate education for boys and girls to Year 10, although I am very aware that I am a minority voter in that area.

Paradoxically, it has been established that boys educated at 'Greater Public Schools'—single sex schools, attainable only for the rich and privileged—often have the most intolerable attitudes towards women and girls. There are suggestions—which I endorse—proposing a balance of female and male principals and senior staff at such colleges. At the same time, let the exclusive girls colleges recruit more and better trained male staff. Equality must become the norm in all areas of life, especially in politics and business.

As I matured, I became aware of the differences and fallibilities of men and women, but it was apparent that many men, especially, were duplicitous. I became very conservative around this subject, especially after reading seminal works like *Damned Whores and God's Police* written in 1975 by Anne Summers; that book should be required reading for all teenage boys as a component of the teaching of Ethics, commencing from Day One of pre-school. I advocate similar teaching for girls. An important component of Ethics courses should be an admixture of female and male teachers organising healthy discussion at all times.

> **There is no doubt that male members of the human species, by and large, are physically stronger than females, but that does not give men any right to dominate or exploit women.**

There is no doubt that male members of the human species, by and large, are physically stronger than females, but that does not give men any right to dominate or exploit women. I advocate 'naming and shaming' of all males who transgress this principle, with the prospect of serious terms of imprisonment. Further, I support the notion of chemical castration of serial male sexual offenders, on the recommendation of a panel of female and male judges. We don't hesitate to treat intransigent animals—or those deemed unsuitable for breeding—in this manner. There is a basic assumption that human societal standards necessarily get better as time goes by. I do not agree.

Because of deplorable, exploitative behaviour at all levels of society, extending to state and federal parliaments, Australians have become conscious in recent years of the need to promote what is being called 'gender equality', hopefully leading as a consequence to greater respect for women. There is much more to it than preaching 'equality': affirmative action is required, everywhere. A good way to inhibit harassment is to have gender quotas in political parties and large business endeavours.

Domestic violence is also to be totally abhorred. So often we hear of the perpetration of physical assaults, mental torture, even the murder of partners and children. Again—sadly—I must acknowledge that my fellow males are the worst offenders. It must stop, but men are not likely to be convinced by fancy slogans, demonstrations, or wearing of white ribbons. They must be brought to task and receive appropriate punishment for misdemeanours of course, but surely we must first seek to establish a system whereby potential offenders are aware—at all times and at all levels—of the extent of punishment to expect if they cut loose. Name and shame the thugs. Put their photos in their pubs. Seek public banishment from their sporting clubs.

> Alcohol is correctly blamed for much of the domestic violence that occurs. The adage must apply: 'If alcohol costs more than money, give it a miss.'

Alcohol is correctly blamed for much of the domestic violence that occurs. The adage must apply: 'If alcohol costs more than money, give it a miss'. Particularly, First Australians suffer in these matters. What was once their greatest strength—the kinship system and its concomitant sharing—nowadays leads individuals and communities into tragic binge drinking, where the mindset (demonstrated to them in prohibition times by the whites who controlled their lives) is that alcohol is 'strong stuff', consumed in order to promote and justify aggression and violence. No suggestion of conviviality or purchase of appurtenant food: money is for grog. But don't ring a bell.

We often hear statements that men 'have the right' to physical and sexual 'control' of female partners. I have a good friend who married twice. On both wedding nights she received a black eye, from the new husband, as a warning that henceforth she belonged to him! This is arrant nonsense and must be stamped out by a determined judiciary system. Better men must lead the way here. Again, name and shame offenders.

> We often hear statements that men 'have the right' to physical and sexual 'control' of female partners.

Here are a couple of verses from my song *Survivors*—written for Australian men and women to sing together:

> Let's not forget the courage of sisters who've suffered
> They've been traded, degraded,
> Bashed, deserted and raped.
> Whenever we meet them all damaged and bruised
> Black eyes, busted noses, bloody confused,
> Spirits near-broken, bodies misused
> We must help them escape from it all.
>
> Help them survive, they've had enough
> It's time for all the people of the world
> To show that we are tough.
> The world will hear this call
> Equality for all
> They/we are the women
> They/we will survive.
>
> And don't you forget, all you men who think women are chattels
> The old rule of thumb is repealed
> You're out on a limb.
> You're just bloody mongrels
> With nothing to show
> So I'd like to tell you where you ought to go
> And, when you get there, I'd like you to know
> You're despised and reviled by us all
>
> They will survive
> We've had enough
> Of all the gutless wonders in the world
> Who kid themselves they're tough
> Hear these words of mine
> You wimps without a spine,
> Hands off the women
> They will survive.

> *Final rally*
>
> We/they will survive
> We've all had enough
> It's time for all the people of the world
> To show that we are tough
> The world will hear this call
> Equality for all
> We/they are the women
> We/they will survive
> We/they are the women
> We/they will survive

In adult years I came to recognise gender and sexuality differences. Admirable campaigns brought on the disapproval of pejorative, intolerant nouns and adjectives. Positive alternatives developed. Sadly, the spokespersons for the so-called civilised world—usually shielding behind the man-made protection of various religions—refuse to acknowledge the right of women to equal participation in life, seek to deny the legality of adult same sex relationships. How dare they?

23 Summary and Conclusion

I HOPE I HAVE COVERED GROUND THAT IS IMPORTANT TO ALL Australians at this perilous time. The Covid 19 Pandemic will affect humanity for the rest of my lifetime and probably beyond. Let us hope that we have learned some lessons. We need to be prepared for future universal epidemics, of whatever kind, for the human propensity to travel by the many means available will guarantee the spread of any virus. We must seek to be positive in respect of assembly of crowds at festivals, sporting events. It has been established within Covid 19 that it possible for many people to work effectively at home. Surely, that is good practice in every respect? The principles and methods developed in Distance Education in Australia present the opportunity for training of school teachers who, in turn, can monitor home education of children in emergency situations. Devices like respirators, personal protection equipment (PPE) and the training of appropriate personnel are obviously principal components in the early recognition and treatment of whatever emergency. Quarantining is such an obvious requirement in the event of pandemics that there must be, at all times, appropriate facilities available in strategic places. Be prepared, said Baden Powell.

In my 90th year at this time of reflection, I derive consolation that I have been a beneficiary of the best period Australia will ever offer its citizens.

Born in 1932, I was too young when World War II drastically affected so many promising Australian lives and careers. I was too old for involvement in all subsequent wars. When I left school in 1947, aged fifteen, I could have taken up any one of probably fifty job opportunities, although I had no trade skills, nothing but the piece of paper that said I was well educated, when in reality I had simply been trained to pass the exams. I went to the Northern Territory as a youth: I will almost certainly die there. Life has been good to me in every respect. I keep saying: I have never been happier, never been uglier, never been busier. I will probably die, still advancing 'my good ideas', still seeking understanding. Kulilkatima.

In summary:

- I hope that Australia, post Covid becomes a better nation all round, based principally on gender equality, seeking unity rather than friction in major issues
- I hope we can provide permanent, meaningful sovereignty for First Australians in their designated Heritage Nations.
- I hope we can become a nation that is respected throughout the world as having—as its principal driving force—compassion for our own citizens and all the other residents and creatures living on planet Earth.
- I hope that through sheer hard work, we may create a positive, peaceful future for our young and unborn.
- I hope we remain determined to do all things necessary to effect positive climate change.
- I hope we find the means to love one another, especially in our families.
- I hope that, at all times, we resist rather than condone war or conflict of any kind.
- In that respect, I hope that we avoid alliances that seek to dominate or manipulate us.
- I hope that all forms of division will at all times come under scrutiny.

Summary and Conclusion

- I hope that Australia shines in a viable and healthy planet: Earth.

I am concerned for the future that faces my grandchildren and great grandchildren. I keep telling them that they have "inherited good genes" and, thereby, they have good prospects. I hope that ensues. I wish them well.

In summing up my concerns and hopes for Australia, I am apprehensive and appreciative, concerned yet confident, for I respect and admire the people of my country. I feel that many of us will do staggering things in the testing years ahead.

www.ingramcontent.com/pod-product-compliance
Lightning Source LLC
Chambersburg PA
CBHW042110230426
43662CB00042B/2458